BERLIN WORK
SAMPLERS &
EMBROIDERY
of the Nineteenth Century

Jules David

Raffaella Serena

BERLIN WORK
SAMPLERS &
EMBROIDERY
of the Nineteenth Century

introduction by Marina Carmignani

translated from Italian by Laura M. Dini

LACIS

Page 2: *Two women conversing in front of an embroidery frame*, from "Moniteur de la mode", 1845. Paris, Biblioteque des ArtsDecoratifs.
Page 6: *Inside a jeweller's shop*. Lithograph by Carl Kunze Johan Geiger, 1838. Vienna, Museen der Stadt.
Page 94: Detail of a rug illustrated on page 42.

Translated from the Italian title
a Piccoli Punti
originally published by Istituto Geografico De Agostini, Novara

Credits for Original Edition

Director: Marco Drago, Andrea Boroli
Director of Various Books, Illustrated and Childrens: Marcella Boroli
Editor - in - Chief: Cristina Cappa Legora
Editing Coordinator: Franca Correngia
Editing: Silvia Broggi
Editing Secretary: Maria Pia Arciuli
Graphics: Studio Cree
Graphic Realization: Francesco Viano
Iconographical Research done by Instituto Geografico De Agostini and the Author

Credits for English Language Edition

English translation: Laura M. Dini
Format: Lacis
Support and encouragement: Barbara De Spirt

© 1991 Istituto Geografico De Agostini, Novara
© 1996 Lacis, English text

Publisher's Notes:

The descriptive color names as keyed to the DMC color numbers are as translated from the original Italian edition of this book and do not necessarily reflect the common descriptive names of the colors as recognized in the US. Where appropriate to the context, the archaic English spellings of words have been used.

This edition published jointly by

DMC Corporation
10 Port Kearny
South Kearny, NJ 07032
USA

LACIS
3163 Adeline Street
Berkeley, CA 94703
USA

ISBN 0-916896-66-8

Printed in Hong Kong, 1996

When I think of embroidery I think of Penelope who weaves and then unweaves her loom, patiently absorbed in her work; a long, solitary wait, a discreet unfolding upon itself, her hands that move lightly and quickly, busy in her pleasant work while her mind is free to fantasize or think. Domestic art for excellence, feminine art made of dreams and thoughts, next to an open window to catch the light or near a fire where the flames make colors dance. The technique of the great manufacturers raised embroidery to the highest level of artistic creativity without destroying its intimate character: Aubusson, Beauvais, Le Fiandre, I Gobelins, these famous names hide anonymous craftsmen. They embellished the important households, rich merchants or princes, ambassadors or cardinals; embroidery became regal, writing within its wefts, woven with gold or light blue, lilies or crowns to indicate the owner, protector or patron, contributing in that way to its fame.

In the meantime, the art of the petit point or cross stitch in the intimacy of the bourgeois or upper-class homes, cultivated the secret soul of the tapestry - a world somewhat mysterious with its blue-green leaves and silver reflections, the "greens" that remind one of the French woodlands or the high forests in the Netherlands; the animals, real or imagined of Europe or of the islands, lambs or parrots when there isn't a unicorn following his Lady. The characters could be princes or shepherds, legendary heroes or rosy-cheeked youngsters that gather flowers. Dreamy atmospheres, vaguely nostalgic with sentimental scenes that eternally honor with their fixed smiles the cushions, purses or hand-warmers. One thinks about the dreaming women that, in their boudoir in Florence, near the window of their villa on Lake Maggiore or next to the fireplace of their castle in the Hampshires, weave their dreams with the threads of wool or silk idealizing those precious messages handed down to us. To enter into the magical world of embroidery some wool thread and a needle are enough, a friendly combination between the eye and the hand will bloom with design and colors from the wefts. I hope that this book will help us admire some refined works of a disappearing art; that it will send the message of a living art, testimony to a culture, par excellence from Europe, in which in an epoch tending to forget it, we will remain faithful. I hope that it will inspire continuing the tradition of embroidery and pass the message on...

HUGUETTE PÉROL
Ambassador of France in Rome

Table of Contents

Reflections about Nineteenth Century Embroidery

*T*he material presented in this volume is evidence of the continued interest embroidery generated in the nineteenth century as well as the form and the distinctive character that it assumed throughout this century. The material is presented from the perspective of design, evolution and origin. The variety and homogeneity of previous times poses a number of questions about the historical journey taken by embroidery as well as the reasons for its vast dissemination. It is recognized that, at the threshold of the year two thousand, embroidery is still extremely interesting, continuing to intrigue us and arouse our curiosity.

The vast and fascinating selection of material is essentially divided into two categories: *samplers* - small pieces of embroidery on linen or cotton plain weave fabric, generally worked by young girls at home or at school; and the designs created to be embroidered using *petit point,* a stitch that in the nineteenth century was known as *Berlin Work* - an easy and quick technique, used to make many objects, both personal and domestic.

Of course these examples don't represent the entire production of the nineteenth century but they do show much of the evolution that took place between the eighteenth and nineteenth century in form and techniques as well as in design. Both groups have their own histories that start at the beginning of the sixteenth century. Both also symbolize the fundamental aspect that associates femininity with domestic embroidery which grows and expands, especially in the nineteenth century.

The profound changes begun in previous centuries now reach their maturity. These transformations confirm that this antique and illustrious art is assigned definitely to women, for public production as well as for the home where it will acquire an important place in a woman's daily routine and become a fundamental learning tool. In the nineteenth century women's professional status in the textile field is a

Facing page , a model for a garland, in German the initials of the names of flowers (Fabrita, Rose, Elycrisum, Uvularia, Nelke, Datura, Sonnemblumie, Caprifolium, Hortensia, Amarylies, Flieder, Tulpe) form the word Freundschaft: friendship. Berlin, Kunstbibliothek

9

reality: women replacing the century old figure of the male embroiderer. In fact, women's work is organized quite differently; in private workshops and in the public institutions which are part of the production circuit.

Perhaps precisely because embroidery is now a female craft, many people forget that embroidery, before the nineteenth century, was an antique tradition of high quality and, overall, an all-male field.

Embroiderers enjoyed the same esteem as painters and from the Middle Ages were organized in guilds, obliged to obey strict rules that guaranteed the high quality of the manufactured articles. Some embroidery guilds were closely linked to the art of the silk manufacturers, other guilds were independent[1].

The work was produced in workshops organized by seniority and, since the Middle Ages, used designs created by contemporary artists to illustrate erudite iconographical themes; the lives of saints, popular stories or important symbols...a kind of "painting by needle" that was respected as much as painting itself. One need only remember that during

Pillow - case in white satin, colored silk and gold threads. England, 16th century. London, Victoria and Albert Museum.

10

Sampler in linen, embroidered with silk, metallic threads and small pearls. England, 1598. London, Victoria and Albert Museum.

the Renaissance many artists e.g., Sassetta, Pollaiolo, Bellini, Botticelli, Raffaellino del Garbo, an embroiderer himself, created designs to be used for embroidery.

At that time, women were excluded from the productive process and, except for those rare times when, due to family ties, women were allowed to be present, they always had a minor role. Their collaboration was limited to unimportant tasks such as the preparation of materials; tasks similar to that which were required of the nuns living in the cloistered convents. The trade guilds remained practically unchanged up to the last quarter of the eighteenth century. With the abolishment of these guilds, the figure of the male embroiderer and the production of embroidery was completely handed over to women.

In the nineteenth century embroidery was worked in small and large workshops, in homes, and in convents where the merchants would come to place their orders and pay the modest fees. Embroidery was also performed at home, the women working for various manufacturers. The lack of structured organizations for women who embroidered in the home permitted a type of fragmentation and wide-spread dissemination of this craft.

Demand also changed, concentrating on white embroidery worked on white linens used for the home, lingerie and underclothes for children. Another type of embroidery, also used for household goods, was worked with multi-colored silk threads. There was less demand for the figurative ecclesiastical embroideries which were usually worked in the specialized centers that harked back to illustrious traditions[2]. Even for the church the embroidery that is now made is technically simpler with floral designs popular, similar to the work made for the home.

Domestic Embroidery

For the public markets, embroidery is wholly entrusted to the able hands of women. At home it becomes an essential part of a woman's daily work routine. In the nineteenth century embroidery becomes, whether at home or at school, completely linked to women, taking on the distinct image which embodies the concept of femininity. Within the strict lines of domestic life, embroidery represents many of the virtues regarded as important for women: *patience, precision* and *diligence*. These virtues are part of embroidery work and seem to be fundamental steps for the education and up-bringing of a young girl, who needs to develop these qualities to become a woman, wife and mother and who, at a certain social level, may spend her entire life within the four walls of her home.

In the nineteenth century, sewing, weaving and embroidery clearly become part of the daily routine for women of every social class. These tasks take on moral significance as they are transformed into symbols of femininity. This is part of the role that women were destined to have, a role that is judged to be appropriate to expressing their meek and mild character.

This is true for women everywhere and from all levels of society. These skills become part of the educational curriculum and are taught in virtually every type of girl's school[3], especially those emphasizing the most complete education. The principal rule is always based on *«Order, method, neatness in everything and perfect knowledge of all kinds of household work, exact punctuality, and obedience to the laws of time and place. »*[4].

This principal, particularly evident in the culture of the nineteenth century, had already begun in the sixteenth century. In addition to professional work and that from artist's

Detail of an embroidered border of a hunting scene. England (Sheldon), beginning of the 17th century. London, Victoria and Albert Museum.

13

Detail of an embroidered border of a hunting scene. England (Sheldon), beginning of the 17th century. London, Victoria and Albert Museum.

studios, a very precise phenomenon begins to evolve: -- that of domestic embroidery. Now, a particular process begins in which embroidery becomes an educational activity for women, allowing them to exercise feminine virtue while preparing for other types of work. This process will end within the nineteenth century. Domestic embroidery (the sixteenth century "exploit" is referred to with this term[5]) flourished at the same time in Italy, England and Germany creating from women's irregular handiwork a well organized working method involving a growing number of women that embroider for their own personnel pleasure as well as for profit.

Detail of an embroidered border in multi-colored silk. England, 17th century. London, Victoria and Albert Museum.

15

Cushion embroidered with petit point on linen. England, 17th century. London, Victoria and Albert Museum.

Evidence of the vast scale of this movement in Europe is the simultaneous publication of books full of patterns[6], all addressed to the "Noble and Virtuous Ladies" who require a different embroidery process than that of the professional workshops. These books, simultaneously printed in various countries of Europe, have geometric, floral or animal designs which are also found on many household items. The publications are not only used to spread the use of patterns but also give technical instructions for making the actual embroidery, from the simplest to the most difficult stitches. By the second half of the sixteenth century, when such technical knowledge is more commonly known, these publications become progressively less technical in their content. Contemporary literature supports this new feminine occupation that, even from its sporadic beginnings, seems to have become quite substantial and widespread. In fact, there are various texts in the sixteenth century that suggest that among the proper behavior patterns fit for a young girl, all handiwork with a needle should be used not only to keep

CAMPDEN NEEDLECRAFT CENTRE

Helen Kirkup owner/founder of the Campden Needlecraft Centre in Chipping Campden is retiring this Autumn 2002 and closing the shop after 30 years.

OUR RETIREMENT SALE

Starts 20 July 2002

This will be a unique opportunity to browse through the extensive stock of this renowned embroidery shop for the last time and buy your goods at much reduced prices. Huge ranges of threads and fabrics, kits and leaflets – all our stock must go by the end of September. Reductions for postal customers too though a personal visit really is *"a must"*.

We would like to thank all our customers who have supported us so loyally over the years and do hope we will have a chance to say 'goodbye' personally before we close.

Chipping Campden, Gloucestershire GL55 6AG
Tel: 01386 840583   Fax: 01386 841 442
e-mail: needlecraft@chipping-campden.freeserve.co.uk

Sampler in linen, embroidered in silk and metallic thread. England, first half of the XVIIth century. Often these small designs were embroidered on thin material and then cut out and put onto clothes, curtains for canopy beds...generally in velvet. London, Victoria and Albert Museum.

Embroidered panel in petit point with a vase of flowers. England, beginning of the XVIIIth century. London, Victoria and Albert Museum.

one busy but also as an exercise of virtue[7].

Frequently there are references made to the images of ancient Penelope and Aracne, and with these images certain associations develop which reach the height of expression in the nineteenth century, images *representing patience, precision, perseverance and virtue,* all considered exemplary of the feminine nature. Already in the sixteenth century the exact definition of this nature becomes clearer in the institutions that represent an educational function: the convents. Later on, the all-girl schools also incorporate needle-work as one of the fundamental necessities in the preparation of a young girl's life.

It was a type of responsible training: for rich girls, excluded from the work world, it would suffice to learn how to run their own household once they were married; for less affluent girls with the same education, this training gave them the opportunity to earn their living. Starting in the sixteenth century and continuing well into the nineteenth century, this dual system of education plus the preparation for work, guaranteed a constant interest in embroidery and also simultaneously prepared an always increasing number of embroideresses. This fact is made evident by the exceptional flowering of new *samplers* and pieces worked in *petit point*.

Sampler in linen, embroidered in various colors of silk. England, beginning of the XVIII century. London, Victoria and Albert Museum.

Samplers

The embroidered sampler, realizing its double function of education and preparation for work, begins to alter its original, strictly functional, structure. In fact, embroiderers had always used pieces of linen, to practice their techniques, make sketches, and experiment with design and color changes as necessary for the creation of the final embroidery. They would also record ideas for a future piece[8] in this same manner.

In the sixteenth century the working of these small pieces assumes a specific and precise role. A small piece, often made

Sampler with letters of the alphabet, letters, borders, floral designs and embroidery trials done in various stitches. Embroidered in silk thread on a dense linen, 14" x 10-1/2 in. Bohemia, 1801. Florence, Palazzo Davanzati.

Embroidered in cross stitch on ecru linen. Second half of the XIXth century. Florence, Palazzo Davanzati.

by young men and women between the ages of 5 and 17 to learn how to embroider, soon became a way of learning moral values. In the rare examples that survived from the sixteenth century, the individual character of the sample is obvious. After 1636[9], when these works are done in a scholastic setting, the dimensions of the cloth designs, stitches and the type of chromatic range follow more precisely the rigid criteria of a well organized and structured curriculum.

The lines of letters of the alphabet and numbers become not only consistently used for practice but also to mark household linens, the signature, that makes an object customized. Likewise, embroidery is used to create the religious symbols

Embroidered chair in petit point on hemp cloth. The theme, the poet and the rose is taken from the fairy tale of John Gay, illustrated by William Kent. England, circa 1730. London, Victoria and Albert Museum.

and the long reproductions of biblical stories as well as the profound contemplations on the meaning of life, as chosen for their wisdom and insight. All intended to heavily influence the young student's ideas with respect to religion, ethics and domestic affairs.

Each country, in Europe as in America, inserts into the *samplers* part of its own traditions, creating a continual modification in the types of designs, the places of work, the general layout and the chromatic range of threads. All these variations are keys to placement as to origin and date. But no place and no school ever loses sight of the final goal well characterized in 1675 by Thomas Brook: *«It is that learning to write is also learning to live»*[10].

These variations in design, combined with new social and economic progress, sees a continual growth of all types of personal and household linens. This type of work, imposed by sixteenth and seventeenth century fashion, has a definite influence on the technique of embroidery. No longer destined exclusively for the rich and the important ecclesiastical furnishings, now it is also used to add grace to the more traditional figurative items, previously very severe and solemn. The incorporation of more complex geometric designs, plants, flowers or images, not much different from those found in the books of patterns, becomes popular.

Petit Point

Similar aspects, as attached to the *samplers*, particularly from the sixteenth century on, are evident with the exceptional growth of *petit point*. Because of its technical characteristics, *petit point* holds an interest for professional work as well as for woman's domestic work. Known by the French term, *petit point*, it appears elementary[11]. The simple techniques however, don't prevent the realization of many color *nuances* and the capacity for distinctive effects by combining wool, silk and gold threads.

Despite its always being known, the wide spread working of *petit point* occurs the moment in which it is used to imitate the woven tapestry by an easier process. It is, in fact, in the sixteenth century, that together with *petit point*, the Ungaro stitch and the Gobelin stitch (these are equally simple) acquire prominence. The course of the threads change but they obtain a likewise rich and substantial effect. These stitches are perfect for creating door hangings, blankets bed covers, cushions, chair covers, frames and coverings for the inside of furniture and writing desks.

There are many English and French examples from the sixteenth century that illustrate this widespread dissemination and the high

Embroidered chair in petit point on hemp cloth with a scene taken from the fairy tale of John Gay, illustrated by William Kent. England, circa 1730. London, Victoria and Albert Museum.

Sampler with a floral border embroidered with silk threads that encircle various embroidery trials, done by Hannah Haynes. England, 1725-1730. London, Victoria and Albert Museum

quality that was achieved. Requests for these pieces were so extensive that, under the reign of Louis XIVth, the embroiderers were part of the Gobelins manufacture, where the highest quality of design and technique of the manufactured article was highly maintained. In this way *petit point* entered into a work organization that was strengthened by the demands of the court designers and very precise roles were created. For example some embroiderers, like Simon Fayette, specialized in the reproduction of figured embroideries; others, like Filibert Bellard, produced landscapes[12].

Requests for such manufactured articles throughout the seventeenth and eighteenth centuries caused an increase in the number of workshops, some of which, like those started in Saint-Cyr by Madam of Maintenon, distinguished themselves for their high quality. Encouragement to develop *quality* embroidery was not only from the suggestion of professional embroiderers but also from the rising number of women who embroidered at home. As a pastime some of these women were able to reproduce with excellent results the most famous pieces for the decoration of their own home,

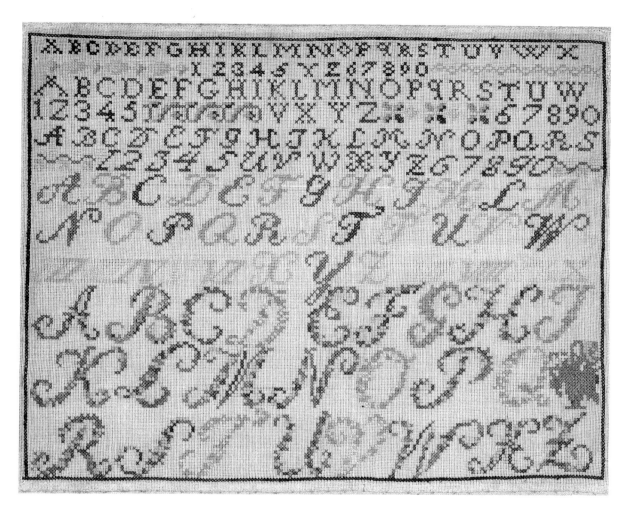

Sampler embroidered in cross stitch on linen cloth with letters of the alphabet and numbers, properly called abc learner. In this way the feminine education in the nineteenth century was based on practicing embroidery and writing. Germany, XIXth century. Hamburg, Museum für Kunst und Gewerbe.

while others worked for outside workshops. From the time when *petit point* first appeared, there were wonderful examples illustrating the domestic application of this stitch. This was the case in Maria Stuarda's court where the women embroidered pillow covers with dates, motto and coat of arms[13].

The decorative repertory is vast; floral designs are common and easily used, as are figured scenes and animals. More complex designs like mythological scenes, court scenes or rural gatherings are easily inserted into the decorative themes of the aristocratic homes of that period, finding a certain homogeneity with the general style of contemporary textile production and applied art.

The Process Simplifies

Sampler embroidered in silk with petit point and cross stitch on linen salmon color, 16" x 20-1/2", with a typical romantic image. Denmark, 1846. Celle, Das Deutsche Stickmuster Museum.

If the *sampler* and *petit point* represent the confirmation of female progression in the embroidery field and the attributed function of education (characteristics that become predominant in the nineteenth century but start at the beginning of the sixteenth century), then they also effectively demonstrate the quality and stylistic evolution of the art of embroidery. Though the dual role of work and moral teaching remains,

during the nineteenth century a certain deterioration starts to infuse the technical and design quality that had characterized these manufactured articles in the seventeenth and eighteenth centuries.

The changing of work methods marked a simplification of the process, with a corresponding evolution of a style reflecting a connection to social and economic factors.

The technical simplification is specific in both kinds of work. As for the *samplers*, cotton and hemp join the traditional linen cloths and are embroidered almost exclusively in cross stitch and *petit point*. To overcome the limitations of the minor technical ability needed, different from the complex technical ability needed during the seventeenth and eighteenth century, more basic chromatic effects are sought. These are obtained with wool and cotton threads. In 1856 the first synthetically dyed thread is made, certainly more vivid, but because produced by formula, it lost the specific chromatic characteristics that distinguished one region from another.

Less technical ability and imagination characterizes these samplers, by now typical scholastic work, adding little to the rich repertoire of designs (plus the continual variations) that was established in preceding centuries. Inspiration is no longer entrusted to the creative spirit, to the fresh imagination of youngsters or to retrieval of the symbolic heritage of each country. Now teachers easily refer to the student texts for source material and the same poems and designs are identically reproduced everywhere.

Thus, from the beginning of the nineteenth century, a more homogeneous production is seen, as might be anticipated. These pieces now concentrate above all on lines of numbers and letters of the alphabet, moral thoughts and some religious symbols.

Berlin work

While the creation of *samplers* in the schools continues up until the twentieth century, its decline actually goes back to the middle of the nineteenth century (there are, of course, some important examples seeming to contradict this general tendency). This is when new forms of work, together with modern technical inventions, begin to spread, with significant changes to *petit point* as part of this transition.

In the nineteenth century the name also changes, *petit point* becoming referred to throughout all of Europe as *Berlin Work*, named for the first published pattern on graphed paper from Berlin in 1804, from the publisher Philisson. This simple innovation, of which this book offers many examples, made the old *petit point* technically easier, now allowing the embroiderer to follow the design from a pattern; each square represen-

Embroidered cushion in wool on hemp cloth. England, the third part of the XVIIIth century. London, Victoria and Albert Museum

29

ting an embroidered stitch.

This tendency to make the work easier and quicker to do was confirmed by the growing manufacture of plain weave cloths (for example Penelope), where the threads were woven in groups of four to ease visual counting and allowing the work to go quickly. In 1851 there was a most significant change with the appearance of pre-sketched cloths[14].

It was this ease of doing the embroidery that lead to the publication and endless repetition of designs, reproduced on a faster industrial level. In 1810, M. Wittich had imported a small quantity of patterns published by Ackerman into England, in 1831 Mrs. Wilks of Regent Street had proof of a substantial business and in 1840, 14,000 patterns were in circulation[15].

The dissemination of this material happens through printed albums of patterns that are in circulation everywhere and through women's magazines, which offer an inexhaustible fountain of hints to satisfy all needs[16]. Above all, from the middle of the century, a level of publication begins that still exists today, that is capable of furnishing models and methods offering everyone the possibility of working in private.

With this uniformity of patterns in circulation and the availability of written instruction, there is not much difference among the pieces that one could buy and those that could be done at home. The possibility of doing three-dimensional designs with one stitch fascinated women of all ages who are enticed not only to embellish objects and small personal accessories (change purses, purses, slippers, tea cozies, bookmarks, book covers and frames), but also to create large pieces and various forms for the decoration of their own intimate, domestic surroundings.

The extraordinary popularity of these works, in Europe as in America, are seen in the frequency with which they are present in the exhibits focusing on women's handiwork that seem to be happening everywhere. If at the beginning of the century women's handiwork finds only a small space in

Sampler embroidered in silk and gold threads on thin linen. It is interesting to note the difference between the top and bottom; the bottom is an organized and diligent sample of stitches and the top is a unstructured blend of designs from the author fantasy. Germany, 1736. Hamburg, Museum für Kunst und Gewerbe.

Sampler embroidered in cross stitch in silk on linen, 15-3/4" x 15-1/4", signed by the author, F.C. Meyer. Southern Germany, circa 1820. Celle, Das Deutsche Stickmuster Museum.

the European exhibits, progressively they acquire enough interest to have their own exhibits, actual *Exhibits for Domestic Households*[17], evidence of the growth of this phenomenon from the view of general enjoyment, as well as evidence of the widespread dissemination of certain styles. These exhibits also serve as a measure of the development of the home industry, and the return of the *small entrepreneur.*

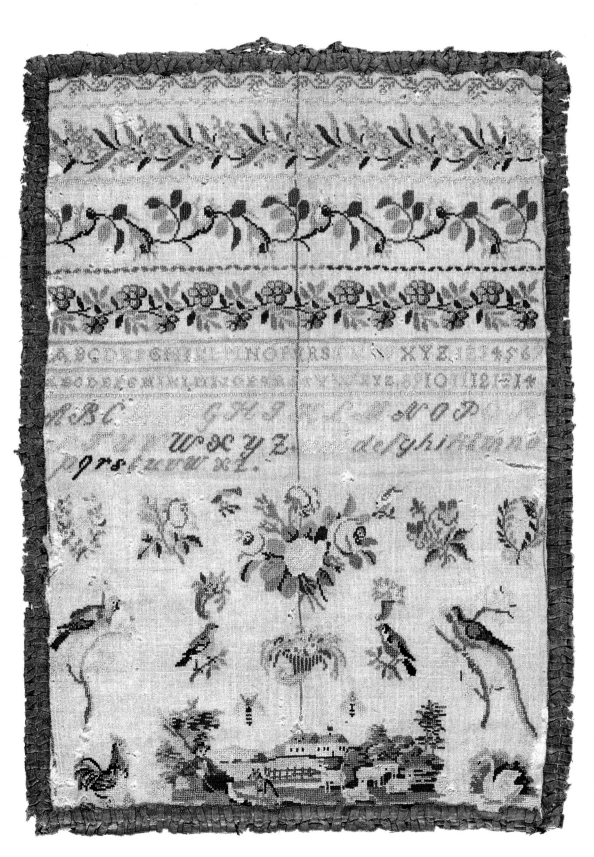

Sampler embroidered with cross stitch on white linen, rich of small motifs and bordered with a fuchsia colored silk ribbon, 15-3/4" x 11.5" Germany, 1821. Celle, Das Deutsche Stickmuster Museum.

Decorative Motifs

If this material shows complex social-economic journeys, it is no less intimately connected to the problem of decoration in the nineteenth century. The designs referred to from the nineteenth century (those illustrated in this book are in this sense particularly important) mirror the bourgeois tone of life and their furnishings. The end of the First Empire was the

Sampler embroidered with cross stitch on a fine weft linen in a limited range of colors. Germany, 1822. Altona, Hamburg, Altonaer Museum.

end of the last court able to instill a homogeneous style encompassing all fields of art. The new and rich bourgeois now begin to have their own style, created with a mixture of a functional yet comfortable association with the nostalgia of all the past styles that expressed the aristocratic way of life. In the small and private surroundings of the nineteenth century households, in the small work rooms and less formal sitting rooms, embroidered pieces, all often decorated with

Embroidered with glass pearls on cloth. 16.5" x 13-3/4" The sixteen squares have figures dressed in regional costumes the whole piece enclosed with the traditional greek design and separated by green floral motifs. Italy, first quarter of the XIXth century. Florence, Palazzo Davanzati.

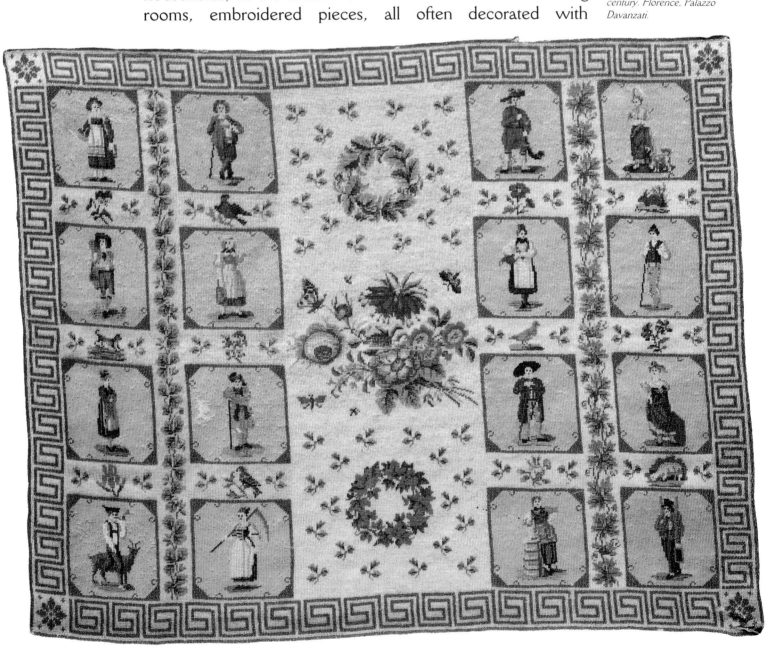

Sampler embroidered in wool on cotton fabric, 16" x 16". Celle, Das Deutsche Stickmuster Museum.

naturalistic flowers, fit well; as framed pieces with nature or other typical scenes, covers, symmetrically placed cushions on couches, door covers, billiard table covers, fire screens, and wall panels.

The idea of a matching and harmonistic style has certainly changed and the elegant and sumptuous emphasizing motifs, that are singularly useful for accentuating overall elegance, disappears. Now, from the inside of the home, there emerges the taste of small, sweet things -- a blooming bouquet, a happy picture of childhood, the simple pleasures of life. All of the elements that emphasize not an elegant appearance, which the past century coveted so highly, but the subtle tones of the bourgeois that dream about the harmony of domestic life. The designs for *petit point* confirm the concentration of floral arrangements -- garlands, bouquets and ribbons poetically winding around branches. These decorative designs are a repeat of the motifs that had formed the seventeenth and eighteenth century vocabulary, restored according to the taste of *revival* that characterizes the culture of this century. It's not difficult to retrace, in the baskets from which flow the large, naturalistic variety of flowers, the original idea begun in the eighteenth century, from court designer Pierre Ranson or in the variety of ribbons and laurel crowns of the famous Philippe de La Salle that had so much influence on nineteenth century textile production, as well as every other type of applied art[18].

Within the theme of harmony that, in substance, doesn't change, are various forms: different kinds of flowers, clusters of grapes and leaves, combinations of colors and precise naturalistic imagery and ribbons that tie together the various elements of the composition. The nineteenth century bourgeoisie was surrounded by a rejoicing of all natural forms. But floral decoration, even if amply used, is not the

Sampler embroidered in silk on linen, 12-1/4" x 19". The inscription, "By S.D.S. Maria Nicolosa of S. Francesco" indicates that this was realized in a convent setting. Italy, 1829. Florence, Palazzo Davanzati.

only form of imagery.

A subject, possibly even more symbolic of this new decorative taste, is that of childhood. An unusual theme that, from the iconographical point of view, was the symbol that the whole century accepted for domestic and familiar subjects. It is, in fact, that during the nineteenth century attention towards the world of childhood is evident with a different image of the child emerging. If the studies of childhood and the discussions on education is the focus of the nineteenth century, then painting and sculpture doesn't grow tired of representing this childhood and the many new aspects that concern it. Very often this subject, as is well documented in the embroideries illustrated on these pages, is shown with such an exaggerated sentimental tone that it is compared to the overly romanticized style of painting and contemporary sculpture.

With embroidery as with painting, other types of pleasant subjects are used; hunting scenes, pleasant outings, domestic conversations, the inevitable dog and the curled up cat.

Even if the quality of the design and subject were not very exceptional they lent themselves to easy and flowing communication. The themes are pleasant and acceptable on all

Facing page: the two sides of a sketch book embroidered with petit point in wool and silk threads on hemp cloth with a leather binding. 6.5" x 3.75" Germany, 1830. Celle, Das Deutsche Stickmuster Museum.

This page: a sampler embroidered in cross stitch in silk on white linen. 12.5" x 19.25" Austria, 1832. Celle, Das Deutsche Stickmuster Museum.

Sampler embroidered in silk with cross stitch and petit point on linen, 11" x 13-5". Italy, first quarter of the XIXth century. Florence, Palazzo Davanzati.

levels, simple and accessible demonstrations of the fundamental points of ethics and style of contemporary life. But this tendency towards a decline in quality didn't discourage the dissemination of these works. Emphasis was on the change of taste of the general decorating style as well as the new themes.

The awareness of the changes, that are introduced by the new social and economic processes, foster discussions on the nature of decoration. The search for a theme that expresses this brilliant tradition but also keeps in mind the new needs of a society that presents itself in a new way, gradually emerges. A necessity already expressed by Ruskin and Pugin finds a precise expression in William Morris with his concern with the renewal of the applied arts; taking into account the overall problem of the requirements of craftsmanship. Morris was especially concerned with embroidery which he felt was an important textile product that could be manufactured of a high quality without losing commercial possibilities. In his factory were such artists as Philip Webb who created motifs for furniture, tiles and embroidery and Burne-Jones[19] who designed motifs for both clerical and home decorations. The quality of the new embroidery makes it harder to reproduce and therefore closer to the finer past traditions. New creations, partly affected by the general trend towards easier techniques, are of various sizes but are preferably large with the favorite subjects,

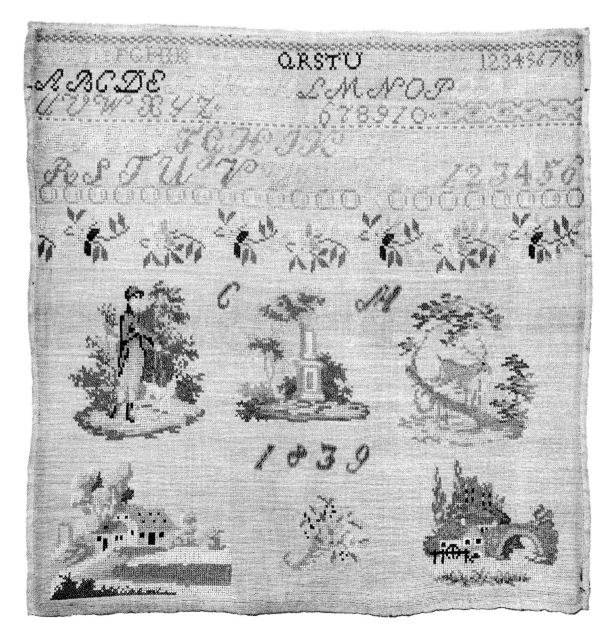

Cross stitched linen sampler embroidered with silk threads. Monogram and date are embroidered with gold colored glass pearls. 13.5" x 13-3/4". Germany, 1839. Celle, Das Deutsche Stickmuster Museum.

flower and human portraits, embroidered with wool and silk threads.

The search for more original pieces is shown by the founding of several European[20] schools focusing on technique and design. These were often annexed to permanent museums which also started collecting masterpieces of applied art. This is of course evidence of a new interest in the production of both modern original work and, at the same time, new interpretations of past themes.

For the first time textile work is both historically and artistically evaluated: public museums and private collections are founded to provide an orderly arrangement of ancient works as well as to promote an awareness of their

Petit point woolen rug made for a wedding celebration and shows a romantic portrait. Garlands are surrounding the bride's and groom's initials and wedding date. France, 1875. Milan. Private Collection.

historical heritage.

The Twentieth Century

While briefly studying the significant events of textile handiwork, we must also look at the present day situation and think about the current course of embroidery. Today the characteristics have changed as have the reasons for these changes. Thanks to women, an antique technical legacy was preserved during the nineteenth century. The process of developing particular social roles that were being newly defined, and the search for a specific vocabulary that responded to necessity and the times, changed. Some of the aspects, duch as the problem of decorative renewal, are still open to change. At the beginning of the twentieth century

Sampler rich with numerous small embroidered designs in cross stitch on very fine linen. France, end of the XIXth century, Paris, Musee´ des Arts Decoratifs

avant-garde artists again try to transfer the latest proposals from modern culture onto embroidery[21].

Another aspect, the association of embroidery to a certain ideal of femininity disappears, giving way to emancipation, which this new century offers to women. It is true that in the twentieth century embroidery is still worked and that, up until about twenty years ago, it was an integral part of the domestic skills taught in the schools. But the form of dual education/work preparation, in which the previous generations were formed, is most certainly gone. This changed the moment women were offered more possibilities in the work force and the possibility of acquiring a more well-rounded culture. This new freedom was already present at the end of the nineteenth century and was the core of this emancipation, often in contrast with the feelings and intolerance of the times.

What surely lasts is the idea of embroidery as a form of expression and individual application. Evidence of this creativity is the growing number of people that are dedicated to embroidery as well the enormous quantity of books that in Europe and America are published in response to public and private demands. The most interesting aspect of this development is that, in this day and age, we can see a definite change in the prejudice that embroidery is "for women only." Finally the shadow of something old and dusty is removed from this illustrious handiwork, it now being created in the light of everyday surroundings.

Rediscovering embroidery are the men, whether for hobby or vocation. There are decorators[22] that personally produce the fabrics that are a part of the furniture that they create. Today there is a complete freedom in design. There are personal ideas and skillful interpretations of Oriental, Victorian and geometric or floral designs with renewed colors and color combinations.

It is certainly not strange that from this creativity, certain ideas for artwork are created. This is the force that pushes these techniques to their full potential, the force, that throughout

Embroidered sampler in cross stitch on linen in an unusual and refined range of colors. The author, Marie Ann, wrote a prayer to Christ. England, middle of the XIXth century. Florence, Palazzo Davanzati.

the centuries, proved to be very flexible to all types of interventions.

There still exists a large number of men and women who embroider and simply want to spend their free time in a relaxing way. To achieve pieces made in good taste they look for inspirations in specialized magazines or in books such as this, that tempt their fantasy. In this way they gather together the experiences, from women as well as men, who, for centuries, have found ways to develop their creative abilities.

MARINA CARMIGNANI

Small purse taken from a collection of embroidery, done in cross stitch on linen. Florence. Palazzo Davanzati.

Notes

1. The situation was different in each country and in each Institute. In Florence for instance, embroiderers at the beginning of the XIVth century were mainly registered in the Art of Por Santa Maria and rarely in the Art of Doctors or Spice Dealers (which also included painters). In Naples, where there was a large number of them, embroiderers had an independent organization, even more active than the one for goldsmiths (quote from M. Carmignani, *Embroidery and lacework in churches and monasteries in Prato between the sixteenth and nineteenth century*, Prato, 1985, page 11-13). In England the first Embroiderers Charta was established in 1561, although other sorts of organized jobs existed before (see G. Winfield Digby, *Elizabethan Embroidery*, London, 1963, page 29 and following).

Detail of a collection of embroidery realized with cross stitch on linen. Florence, Palazzo Davanzati.

2) Clerical embroidery with gold, silver and multicolored silk threads was made at specialized workshops annexed or collaborating with girls' schools. A very typical and interesting example of job organization in the nineteenth century was the workshop in Verona, founded in 1832 at a girl's school started by Don Mazza who also arranged a reliable staff of teachers who worked with contemporary painters for all design matters (see *Don Mazza Canonical Robes. A masterpiece of Silk decoration in Verona*, Mazziana, 1989).

3) Further information can be found in the I. Porciani collection, *Women at School. Women's education in Italy in the nineteenth century*. A documentary and iconographical exhibit which took place in Siena from February 14th until April 26th 1987. The exhibit's catalogue provides a very interesting review of contemporary girls' schools from the common Catholic ones, the aspiring teachers of orphanages and asylums, and the methods that were used in those schools.

4) *The Life of Charlotte Bronte* by E. Gaskell. London, 1961, page 150. Memories of the Bronte sisters who were indeed unusual and exceptional women for their time, are very meaningful and representative of that century.

5) Quoted from *Catalogue of English Domestic Embroidery of the sixteenth and XVIIth centuries*, by J. Nevinson. Victoria and Albert Museum, 1938; also see above mentioned literature by G. Winfield Digby, P. Remington, *English Domestic Needlework of the XVIth, XVIIth and XVIII centuries*, New York, 1945.

6) The first pattern books were edited by Johann Schonsperger in 1523 and were followed by the one of Peter Quentell, edited in Koln in 1527. The first works in Italy were published during the '30s of the sixteenth century by Giovan Antonio Tagliente, Alexandro Paganino and Giovan Andrea Vavassore (called Guadagnino). Shortly thereafter similar works were also published in France and England. The last Italian publication is the one by Catanea Parasole in 1624 following the most famous works of Fredrico Vinciolo in 1606 and Cesare Vecellio in 1617 (see: *Samplers. Needlework practice by European and American young girls between the XVIIth and eighteenth century*, by M. Carmignani, Florence, 1986, page 12 - 13).

7) For instance, Agostino Valier's book, *Life Style Suggestions for Married Ladies*,

Detail of a sampler embroidered in cross stitch on white linen. Germany, 1817. Hamburg, Museum für Kunst und Gewerbe.

from 1560 and then reprinted in Venice 1863, is an invitation to devote themselves to handicrafts. Agostinian Father Jean Baptiste de Glen in his book, *Du Dubvoir des filles,* published in France in 1597 repeats that women of any age and social class should practice *«..l'exercise continuel la bonne et honneste occupation...le labour manuel...affin que telle occupation leur serve de esbort, de plaisir et de delectation honneste pour tromper l'enouy importable que accompagne cette solitude et la vie sedentaire.»*[...continuous exercise of good and earnest occupations...handicraft works...so that such occupations may keep them busy, happy and earnestly entertained during the solitary days of sedentary life.]

8) The habit of using canvas or pieces of fabrics to memorize techniques and designs, is still found in oriental samplers of the XVIIth and nineteenth centuries while the European and American samplers were already independently done.

9) Abstract from *Samplers. Five Centuries of a Gentle Craft,* by A. Sebba, New York, 1979, page 45.

10) Quotation of A. Sebba, page 48 of above mentioned works.

11) *Petit point* is done with a slant stitch but not crossed by a second slant stitch in the opposite direction similar to *gros point* or cross stitch.

12) Quotation from *Ricamo - Italian Encyclopedia,* 29th volume, page 220-230.

13) Quotation from G. Wingfield Digby above mentioned works, page 45.

14) Quotation of M. Carmignani, *Samplers...,* above mentioned works, page 18.

15) Comparison should be done on this matter between M. Proctor's book *Victorian Canvas Work - Berlin Wool Work,* Batsford 1972 and the chapter Berlin Wool Work from *The Larousse Encyclopedia of Embroidery Techniques* by G. Swift, New York, 1984.

16) Starting in the middle of the nineteenth century motifs and patterns were to be found in Italy in such magazines as the *Album dei Lavori e dei Ricami* (Collection of Craft Arts and Embroideries), *Il Ricamo* (Embroidery) or the *Eco della Moda* (Fashion Echo) which usually came with a supplement such as the *Paniere del Lavoro* (Work Basket).

17) Local shows which started in the early nineteenth century were accompanied

by frequent and annual school shows and open houses in several Italian cities where they strictly exhibited the work of schools and professional institutes. The first national show of women's works took place in Florence on March 15th, 1871(see Statistic Directories 1971, page 314)

18) P. Ranson (1736-1786) and P. de La Salle (1723-1805). Their designs are published in M. Abegg text *A propos Patterns for Embroidery, Lace and Woven Textiles*, Bern, 1978.

19) Burne Jones major contribution to embroidery at Morris' workshop was *The Romance of the Rose*, for which he developed paper patterns during the six years from 1874 and 1880. He also produced designs for glass, tiles and clerical embroideries and among them the famous portraits of Saint Cecily and Saint Dorotea (*Textiles by William Morris and Morris & Co.*, by O. Fairclough and E. Learly, 1861 - 1940, London, 1981).

20) The Museum of Manufactures in London was founded in 1852 and was moved to South Kensington in 1857 where it became the center of today's Victoria and Albert Museum, a center for collections and studies of applied arts. The School of Design was founded by Cole in the same spirit as well as the Society of Arts, founded in London in 1855. The Union Centrale Des Beaux Art Applique' a` l'Industrie was founded in 1874 and in 1876 it was the first promoter of a show for qualified art crafts. These are just examples of the various actions that were undertaken at that time to improve applied arts and also life standards especially among the lower social classes.

21) In this respect the efforts of Sonia Delaunay who devoted herself to renewing design for textiles as well as fashion are very significant.

22) We remember among many others Kaffe Fasset, whose works were collected in the book *Glorious Needlepoint*, London, 1987. Candace Bahouth's inspiration was influenced by medieval subjects but he also used petit point to decorate scenes from the modern day world, western as well as eastern. Elisabeth Bradley's works, on the contrary were much influenced by her beloved romantic and Victorian style.

Detail of a cross stitched motif taken from a collection of designs done on white linen. Florence, Palazzo Davanzati.

Chronicle of a discovery:
at the loom, in little shops, in museums of the world

*I*n 1981 I opened, in the heart of old Milan, on Via Lanzone, a few steps from the Basilica of Sant'Ambrogio, The Little Shop of Applied Arts where houses with balconies coexist with noble palaces, close to antique shops and art galleries, where new small artisans' shops open as part of the activities of urban life.

For about ten years I had been painting decorative compositions on blown glass with tempera. I had a workshop equipped at home, and my works had sparked the interest and encouragement of numerous people who had the opportunity to see them. For two years my works had been handled by a Furniture Gallery in New York. Content with these first supportive responses, I decided to open a shop where I could create and exhibit my paintings.

New interests and curiosity encouraged me to continue and try other things and to diversify the activity of the workshop, developing a series, specific to technical crafts and decoration, not necessarily tied to basic painting. These included things such as stenciling and marbling, decorative painting with

Facing page, a detail from a tablecloth for tea, embroidered in cross stitch on white linen. Beginning of the XXth century. Milan, Private Collection.

This page, dance carnet in violet velvet embroidered in multi-colored silk and gold threads. Milan, Private Collection.

masks, prints and marbleizing; and other decorative techniques exemplary of applied arts: figurines in wax from antique prints, decorative boxes and embroidery.

In this field I thought of offering to the public, next to my paintings and other manufactured articles, embroidered cross stitch pieces. For a year I had, from a famous workshop of Italian embroidery, pieces of rare elegance, in terms of the subject matter as well as in their perfect execution. With surprise and disappointment, I found public interest to be very limited.

Back and front of a small purse in silk done in petit point. Milan, Private Collection.

I also, during the pauses of my main activity of glass painting, amused myself embroidering -- reproducing the best designs that I discovered during my searches in the library. However, the major volume of my customers, mostly women, still in a phase of "liberation" and focused towards other objectives, were not interested in embroidery.

The few embroideries sold in that period were acquired by men to give to fortunate women who would have them as companions. I remember one evening a handsome gentleman passing back and forth in front of my shop, quite distinct and with a beard. When he decided to enter he indicated, with a demure and somewhat embarrassed air, that he wanted to acquire an a-b-c learner embroidery piece, asking me to cover the letters from Q to Z. Full of curiosity, I placed as a condition for the sale of my a-b-c learner, that he reveal to me the motive of this unusual request. Reluctantly, he answered that the gift was for a woman that in life had

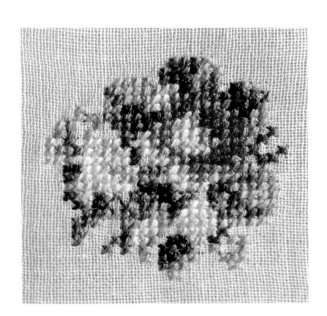

Detail from a baby girls clothing in white linen muslin with small, scattered flower designs in cross stitch. Beginning of the XXth century.

understood only up to the letter Q. I didn't succeed in learning more about this and the bearded gentleman left with his wrapped package without giving other explanations. After some years we became friends; he is still reserved and demure but he no longer has a beard, is happier and has a sweet fiancée.

I thought that, now that we know each other, I could question him about the woman of the letter Q. I succeeded only in learning that they no longer see each other and that the she still had the embroidery. I hope that in the meantime the woman in question has removed the ribbon that covered the other letters of the a-b-c learner and has devoted herself to resolve the mysteries of life that begin with those letters!

Friendly and surprising meetings at tea time

With the many people that frequent the shop, friendships have begun or at least acquaintances. This was certainly the case when I had a workshop at home, where I greeted people in the living room, and invited them to be comfortable, offering tea and appetizer. This often started a pleasant conversation, not necessarily superficial, creating a "hospitable" atmosphere that disguised my nervousness and relaxed the customers.

I understood for the first time the difficult side of this hospitality the day in which an enormous man, similar to Pavarotti, maybe even more imposing, with a thick beard and long, curly hair, wearing an outfit customary to that of a village in the Black Forest, came into the shop. He wore pants that ended at the knee and a black leather suede jacket full of appliqués, a white shirt with lace at the collar which was closed with two enormous red pompons, white socks splendidly interlaced and adorned with tassels and shiny black shoes with heels and a buckle. The image was completed by a feathered hat and a large, gold earring. He had been sent to me by a merchant from Munich in Bavaria, who had ordered some nice glasses about two month before. For a favor to this friend he had decided to personally take on the commission of the delivery.

To thank him for his courtesy I asked him to sit down and offered him something to drink; he chose white wine which was served by a startled waiter from the cafe next door. Meanwhile, in front of the shop, a growing number of curious people stopped and stared, crowding the window, amused and giggling. fascinated by the eccentricities of my guest.

To not embarrass the gentleman, I found an excuse to lower the shutter, staying in the shop with this giant of the forest and a bottle of wine between us. After an hour or so of friendly and agreeable conversation, the gentleman left, with mutual thanks, smiling, and of excellent cheer, passing through the remaining crowd. I asked myself what they all could have been thinking for the time that my visitor and I were inside and they waited outside.

In nine years of my establish-ment there have been many eccentric characters and exceptional stories but many more meetings with

Fine embroidery in silk on tulle in petit point. The picture in the middle is in paper. XIXth century. Milan. Private Collection.

Small purse embroidered with glass pearls with a Greek border, a garland in the middle and the initials of the owner on the latch. Beginning of the XXth century. Milan, Private Collection.

simply nice, pleasant and interesting people -- people from whom I have learned many things, that live in their own right, gifted with the sensibility and intelligence necessary to grow within their personality, with a sense of being, with taste, but also with intellectual spontaneity and creativity.

The first time that she entered my shop she impressed me: a tall woman, distinct, with splendid and intelligent blue eyes, a beautiful aquiline nose, wry smile, fair hair, reserved elegance, and no brand name fashion clothes -- she had the air of a person who has control over her life.

I admired the style and the personality of this woman, full of interests, and I think that we were immediately united by our common taste. She had a passion for embroidery, for the nineteenth-century pieces and for some of the Victorian objects of taste that she had the pleasure of often discovering in my shop. When she comes, I know in advance what she will like and buy, and I enjoy seeing her look around. She immediately finds the object of choice when she enters but, showing perfect self-control, she examines everything without ever losing sight of that which she really is interested in. She then calmly buys it, while a light in her eyes betrays her enthusiasm for this discovery or for the embroidery kit which, I am certain, she will begin to work the minute she is home.

Meeting Gulia, who was then around twenty years old, was an important meeting from a personal as well as a business point of view. A lovely, tall, blonde Anglo-Saxon, she has an angelic face that hides a particularly determined personality. She first came into my shop attracted by an embroidery with a bird and, finding it a bit expensive, asked if she could copy it. I consented, and the following day she returned with the colored pencils to copy the sketch. She fell in love with embroidery and now is quite talented. Despite the age difference, a great friendship began plus an amazing affinity to good taste. Gulia loved my shop and in her time free from studying, she often came to help me.

We have created some very beautiful things together including unforgettable displays. The people passing by would often photograph our front window and whoever visited the shop remained spellbound by the idyllic atmosphere created from the decorations and the presentation of objects. I have gone with Gulia on many trips in the search of exceptional and precious objects and interesting embroideries. Traveling throughout Europe, we have visited most small and large museums, fairs and shows. All the illustrated material published in this volume is the fruit of a long search, in which Gulia has often been my companion, encouraged by her passion for embroidery.

After receiving a brilliant degree in math Gulia worked for more than two years in a multinational company that produces computers, doing such rigid and schematic work that her imagination and intellectual vivacity could not be fully satisfied.

She now is twenty-seven, recently married and has returned to collaborate with me in the shop on Via Lanzone, attracted by the atmosphere of the distinctive surroundings. Today, also thanks to her acquaintance in the computer field, she has helped me with the preparation of my *kits,* making them more functional and "modern," using her imagination in more unrestricted ways.

Detail of a tablecloth for tea with a bunch of poppies embroidered in cross stitch on fine white linen. The rich range of colors allows for an extraordinary softness in the design. Milan, Private Collection.

Small purse with glass pearls in vivid range of colors. End of the XIXth century. Milan, Private Collection.

The first exhibit: Opening Grandmother's Wooden Chest

The initial lack of interest from the public for embroidery did not discourage me. I found these precious works fascinating -- the style and techniques, the beauty in the colors and the equilibrium in the composition. In the meantime I continued to educate myself, completely and profoundly, by acquiring books and visiting museums that have collections of decorative arts and embroideries in particular. Among the many marvelous things that I discovered, were the *samplers* which I have always been attracted to. I returned to London and the Victoria and Albert Museum to see again the precious and bountiful collection of *samplers* that they have. I devoted many hours studying these works, which had for me a distinctive value in evoking a previous time, significant for women. The image of the girls who created these distinctive embroideries has always inspired tenderness. They began to practice needlework very young, with patience and diligence, facing an exercise that was looked upon as fundamental for the education of women, at an age when playing should be the only rule of life. The educational concept that is ideally at the core of these works is actually very distant from the principles and actual methods. Maybe this distance increases the fascination of samplers; on one side exercises on how to embroider, on the other to learn how to read and write the alphabet and numbers. Considering these works under this light could lead us to new realizations and emotions, about life and living, on learning the methods and the pastimes in use in a period not

Business card case in velvet with embroidery in silk on satin. 1875. Milan, Private Collection.

actually very distant from ours. The desire to demonstrate to others my enthusiasm inspired me to take a new direction -- to organize a show of embroidery and cross stitch, many of the pieces being the samplers that I had on loan from a Danish firm and from some Milanese collectors.

In those years I didn't know what a newsletter was or how to write one. I sent invites to all the usual customers of my shop and wrote a letter to the daily newspapers begging the various editors of this sector to publish an announcement of this show and what it was about. Many ignored the plea but some, instead of simply publishing the dates of my small show, were generous, writing brief ads cheerfully announcing "that in Via Lanzone at The Shop of Applied Arts, grandmother's trunk had been opened and old embroideries, curtains, crochet work, household linens and underwear had been found." A banal terminology together with the improbable use of *grandmother*, an example of a certain journalism that uses such stereotypes. For an important wardrobe from the sixteenth century the journalist would undoubtedly refer to it as something from "Grand-mother's Closet!" If only my neighboring antique dealers knew of this insensitivity.

Firescreen: the design, embroidered with glass pearls on linen, is framed in a classical styled temple. France, middle of the XIXth century. Milan, Private Collection.

I would have naturally pre-ferred that the focus would be on the orig-inality of the research, accentuated with the at-tempt of presenting to the public, works in which it was pos-sible to witness the historical and cultural aspects of female daily life and education in the eighteenth and nineteenth centuries.

The successful outcome owes much credit to an article from journalist Marilea Somar which certainly contributed to the overwhelming number of people coming to the shop. Gulia and I carefully studied the display of the pieces and the layout of the exhibition hoping that the sight of the embroideries would arouse not only admiration and tenderness for these works done by children, but also, for some, a desire to embroider.

Embroidered cushion in wool done in petit point with a hunting trophy taken from a design from the XIXth century. Florence, Private Collection.

Today embroidery is no longer part of female education and, not being required, is worked only of free choice. One embroiders for pleasure, to spend hours relaxing, giving the mind freedom from worrying thoughts, and allowing the hands, with needle, colored threads and wool, to create pleasant compositions, in quickly passing time, and in a relaxed and organized flow. Often those that devote themselves to this type of work are not those who have free time but those who have busy and stressful lives. The quiet attention and necessary patience for embroidery is the perfect antidote to an accelerated rhythm of daily life, aspects that are more appreciated by women and less so by men.

The cross stitch and half stitch -- the two being similar because they are the base stitch -- are both extremely easy to learn. The linen or hemp cloth which one uses is often small, making it easy to take everywhere: embroidery lending itself to being a pleasant traveling companion.

The success of the show rekindled my enthusiasm and I began to offer in the shop complete kits, with everything necessary to create an embroidery, almost always reproductions of antique samplers. I brought in supplies from countries in which this tradition was never overlooked, mainly Denmark and England. In Italy such a tradition never took hold and so when I went to introduce this idea, I limited it to patterns and kits in *petit point*. The printed cloth designs, produced in foreign countries, originally France, were mainly of repetitive, common and uninteresting subjects. I selected my patterns, with care and distinctive taste, searching out exceptional, fanciful subjects, attractive for their form or image, for those interested in *cross stitch*, an embroidery technique little known in Italy.

The mystery of the cross stitch

Many asked me to hold courses in cross stitch, not because it presents distinctive difficulties on the front side of the work but because of the difficulty in obtaining a clean reverse side. To have the threads hopefully appearing like small parallel and lined up segments, without knots or tangles of threads that run all over, is a whole different matter! Very few knew how to accomplish this and I knew of only one place where this perfection could be found: a famous workshop of Italian embroidery. With enthusiasm I asked the director of that workshop, a distinguished person, if one of their workers could come to Milan once a week to hold a series of lessons in my shop.

Detail of a floral design embroidered in cross stitch on a baby's outfit in white linen muslin. Beginning of the XXth century. Milan, Private Collection.

I guaranteed a comfortable setting and an adequate salary.

I explained that my intent was not for profit but only the sincere interest to keep alive the desire of continuing a tradition and of spreading this perfect technique. I didn't ask for patterns or designs, of which they had a beautiful and precious collection, but to only learn the knowledge of the technique in order to teach.

The response was a kind denial without a chance for an appeal: the secret of those perfect stitches on the reverse side of their embroidery work would have died with them and their "examples" of cross stitch would stay hermetically closed in an impassable cage of small X's! Finding excitement and challenge facing this difficulty I decided to learn the technique in any way I could and then teach it to others. After spending countless hours with friends, mothers, grandmothers, aunts, and relatives of friends, without result, I decided to turn to the convents.

Top photo, a wide strip, probably used as a napkin carrier, embroidered in petit point on tulle with the initials in gold glass pearls. The border is done in blue, red and green chenille. Lower photo, another wide strip, embroidered in silk and gold on white satin with a green and ecru chenille border. Milan, Private Collection.

Here the real perplexity began: the best teachers of embroidery, offering therefore, the possibility of learning the secret of this distinctive technique, are generally the cloistered nuns. Between them and the world, thus between them and I, there was the famous "curtain" that prevented me from seeing my interlocutor, to understand her instructions, or to understand the secret path of the needle and thread. I pleaded with the nuns to come out of that absurd "booth" but to no avail. The discussion about embroidery became more lively and then moved on to the reasons of that infuriating isolation, a way of living that seemed incomprehensible to me, especially as it pushed me away from my objective. I left those meetings very fidgety and aware of being followed by the detached smile of that invisible embroideress. Among my

Panorama by the lake embroidered in petit point on linen, probably taken from a water-colored painting. Varese, Private Collection.

many impassive victims was a nun, who was a cousin of my father, named Agostina. She was now living in a convent in Abruzzo, in a town by the sea where she had been a teacher and a good embroideress. I began to travel between Milan and Teramo, where my parents live for a few months a year and I was able to obtain from the Mother Superior the permission to have Agostina spend a day with the family during which we could embroider with calm. The nun was very experienced, but because I was not able to follow her, I left convinced that she would never be able to communicate this "technique" to me. I realized later that it is not easy to find a universal code or a fixed rule for this technique because each motif...each design requires different solutions. Together we tried, till the lunch hour, when, from that moment on, embroidery was no longer spoken of. I was anxious to return to work but the nun, after an excellent lunch that my mother had made, lingered at the table chatting, happily and joyfully asking news of relatives and friends. In the end she wanted to enjoy this day with the family, completely forgetting the purpose of her arrival. Once again disappointed, and aware of having wasted my time, I returned to Milan.

I was almost disheartened, losing all hope of being able to resolve the mystery of the cross stitch, when one evening, in the spring of 1986, my husband told me, rather annoyed, that the firm for which he worked had entrusted to him an assignment in London lasting for four or five months. He was sorry, regretting that he would have to leave the family for so much time. I reassured him immediately, suggesting that there would not have to be a separation since we would all gladly come along.

Within a few days a friend in London had found us excellent housing in the heart of the city. I closed my shop in Milan, posting a sign on the window stating that I would "reopen in the autumn." Within one week the whole family was moved to London. My husband didn't face our stay in London happily and was confounded by the promptness with which we had all abandoned Milan. Our son Ugo was very upset, having left all his friends and his girlfriend in Milan. He also had to attend an English school where I had enrolled him, much to his dismay. But I was quite happy; I could calmly visit all of the marvelous museums and maybe, after all my disappointments, attend the Royal School of Needlework to learn the perfect cross stitch technique.

An Unforgettable Experience

In Princess Gate, behind the Victoria and Albert Museum and in front of Kensington Park, lies the Royal School of Needlework. I had never seen a place which so fully embodied the Britannic spirit in every sense. It is a white antique palace with a pillar and a waving flag of the school emblem. The interior is not particularly attractive but still quite suggestive: the ground floor rooms decorated with oak wood wainscots, lacunar ceilings with elaborate golden engravings and a beautiful terrace with a double set of stairs overlooking a garden. In the lobby and foyer, which is connected to the upper floor by an enormous staircase leading to where the workshops are situated, various marvelous embroidered works are displayed in glass cases. They are some of the most

Detail from a baby girl's outfit in white linen muslin, embroidered with cross stitch motifs. Milan, Private Collection.

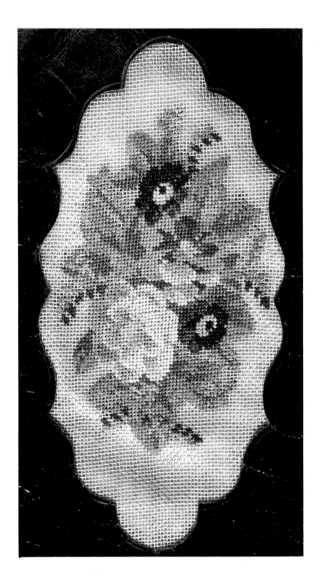

Leather wallet with embroidery in petit point on linen. Florence, Private Collection.

beautiful pieces that been created in the school throughout the years. In an antique cabinet, books on embroidery from every country are displayed next to beautiful linens. For five dollars a week the school "rented out" beautifully embroidered antique linens or canvases which could then be copied and studied before being returned. In another large room it was possible to buy all the necessary materials for embroidering. The variety of materials available was infinite and all the objects were of the finest quality; from the scissors to the thimbles, to the needle cases, boxes and great variety of embroidery kits. In another impressive, lavishly decorated setting, embroidery courses were held. American, Japanese and women from all over the world attended these courses for two year periods. Each and every Wednesday entry was permitted to those who were not enrolled. One could attend a one-hour embroidery lesson or an all day private lesson on a specific project.

The remarkable employees, elderly women in antique clothing, carefully arranged hair and powdered faces, who seemed to have grown up in these unusual surroundings, rendered this place unique:. They conjured up images of magical places from long ago, completely removed from everyday reality. Apart from any personal interest in embroidery, anyone able to capture the spirit of this place could not possibly dislike it. One Wednesday, I enthusiastically attended a lesson for the first time. I brought

Pin cushion in violet velvet decorated with a silk embroidery on pearl colored satin. Valenciennes lace and gold thread. Milan. Private Collection.

with me the embroidered piece created in the famous Italian laboratory previously mentioned. I explained to the teacher that my goal was to learn how to create a perfect cross stitch piece similar to my sample. My disappointment came when I realized that the teacher knew less than I and that those two expensive hours were useless. I then began to search for the addresses of the different specialized museums and conservators of antique embroidery but found the data incomplete and contradictory. With the suggestion of the Craft Council I went to the Docks, a small village where I was told that a group of intellectuals lived who had rediscovered the pleasure of using one's hands. They offered useless conversation about spools of thread for tapestries of questionable taste and other monstrosities. Even there I spent over seventy five dollars without learning anything.

Next I made an appointment to visit Hampton Court. It is the famous castle of Henry VIII where, under the rule of the queen of England, certain lucky women graciously live and work with embroidery. They sell books, organize exhibitions and make use of a vast and rich collection of cross stitch patterns from all over the world. I was greeted kindly by the director and, after she admired the specific piece brought with me, I indicated that I wanted to see if there was a piece created as perfectly in their collections.

She began opening large and small boxes but, after careful examination, much to her surprise and my frustration, there was no work to be considered at the superior level of the craftsmanship of my sample.

I won't talk about the other stops during my research. I just want to remember the kindness of a certain English woman, whom I met by chance. She was the owner of a boutique in

Above, the front and below, the back of a small purse embroidered in glass pearls. Milan, Private Collection.

which she collected and sold beautiful doll houses and miniature furniture. She invited me to her home in a section of Kensington High Street at tea time. There, a big surprise awaited me. My host had invited some of her friends and neighbors who were experienced in cross stitch and who might be able to offer some information. Each one came with her work basket filled with books, needles, linen fabrics, and dressed elegantly in old-fashioned clothing in pastels or floral prints. Although none was able to create a perfect work, I had a pleasant afternoon. Before saying good-bye, I was invited to visit their homes and gardens.

Another interesting encounter, although irrelevant to my purposes, was with a lovely Danish woman, an ardent admirer of Pavarotti. In terms of embroidery, the meeting was a disaster but we entertained ourselves until the afternoon talking about Pavarotti. She asked me specific questions which only those who closely follow him could answer. In order not to delude her I made up creative answers. She was very happy to learn so many details about her idol's life and when I was leaving, she begged me to send him her regards.

During that time, the marriage of Andrew and Sarah, the Dukes of York, was being celebrated. On the occasion the city scheduled many public events in their honor.

The Royal School of Needlework organized an embroidery exhibit made up of pieces created over the course of many years for the Royal English Household. Naturally, I visited this lavish exhibit which displayed some exceptional pieces. In the many rooms were distinctive elderly women who received the visitors and, with watchful eyes, offered information and supervised the outcome of the celebration. I was reprimanded by a kind woman because I was touching various displayed pieces. She asked why I was examining them from the reverse side and I told her that I wished to see if they were well made. She proudly responded by saying that she was certain they were since they were made by the Royal School of Needlework.

Detail from a fire screen embroidered in petit point on very fine linen. Middle of the XIXth century. Milan, Private Collection.

I then extracted my indispensable sample from my purse and also the one I had made during the disappointing two-hour lesson on Wednesday. I explained that at the Royal School I had not learned anything other than the already familiar technique. The woman became pale, then red beneath the layer of white powder. She took my phone number and called me three days later to inform me of a teacher from the Royal School of Needlework who was waiting to give me all the necessary lessons. I kept the appointment and after an hour, despite the difficulties with the diverse methods for each figure or pattern, I finally began to understand. The cloud that was blocking my vision suddenly lifted and the mosaic of information from the many different teachers, the nun and all the people whom I had asked for advice, fell into place.

Detail of a small purse in series embroidered on white silk moire' with silk ribbons and copper paillettes. Venice, XVIIIth century. Milan, Private Collection.

I presently hold courses in my little shop in cross stitch according to a specific method organized by me. At first the students are taught basic technique, but I must say that after eight lessons, they are capable of creating perfect works like the ones from the famous workshop where this long story began.

The Beginning of a Search

At the height of my passion for embroidery, I felt around me a renewed interest in the decorative arts, noticing, as I looked through illustrated magazine articles, a focus on embroidery, lace, and fabrics in particularly inviting environments. The public began to express a surprising interest in cross stitch and *petit point* embroidery with patterns and kits becoming more sought after. This encouraged me to begin a lengthy research project in all the libraries and museums of Europe. In 1989, after having compiled a list of special collections with Gulia, I was ready to depart. The vast amount of material available was an incentive to chronologically broaden my research to the nineteenth century, specifically to the *samplers* and *petit point* embroidery patterns from Berlin. Gulia wrote to all the museums that had collections of this kind, collections generally not publicly exhibited, to ask permission to see them. The responses were mostly positive, the directors expressing enthusiasm and their willingness to make their hidden treasures available for examination.

Florence, Palazzo Davanzati Museum

My first destination was Florence and the renowned Palazzo Davanzati Museum, a perfectly conserved Renaissance type environment full of treasures.

The textile exhibits were diverse. An exposition was held from June to November of 1986 dedicated to an unusual theme: "Samplers." Doctor Maria Todorow, the director, writes in the preface of the catalog: «This is the first Italian exhibit which shows the public and scholars proof of the apprenticeship of children and young adults who worked in Europe and America, at school and at home, from the late sixteenth century to less than 100 years ago».

In addition, it is written: «The collection of samplers conserved in Palazzo Davanzati presently contains about 130 pieces made from the late seventeenth to the late nineteenth century in various parts of Europe and America. This is only a small part of the large collection of 1200 pieces, put together in the last quarter of the nineteenth century by Marshal and Helen Cutler of Boston who moved to Florence in 1890.

The heir to the collection, their daughter Lezley Cutler Girard, donated part of it to the Red Cross in Florence for beneficial purposes. In 1972, the Italian government acquired 97 pieces which made up the initial nucleus of the Palazzo Davanzati collection».

In 1986, the Italian Cassa di Risparmio bank of Florence obtained from the Red Cross an additional 39 *samplers* which they gave

Abc learner enclosed with a border of naturalistic branches, signed on the bottom by the authoress, Magdalena Velasco. It is embroidered in cross stitch on hemp fabric. Italy, second half of XIXth century. Florence, Palazzo Davanzati.

Detail of a sampler embroidered in silk cross stitch on linen fabric. Italy, middle of the XIXth century. Florence, Palazzo Davanzati.

on loan to Palazzo Davanzati Museum. It was not possible for me to see the exhibit because at that time I lived in London, but later, thanks to the kindness and availability of Dr. Maria Fossi Todorow, it was possible for me to admire the incredible collection.

Some Italian samplers were also included and after obtaining the proper authorization from the *Sopraintendenza alla Belle Arti di Firenze* I had some photographs taken. In selecting, I followed a purely aesthetic criteria and I chose only those samplers which seemed not only more significant but also more beautiful.

The Italian samplers seemed less schematic than those of other countries. The choice of subject matter seemed less traditional and they were, therefore, more free in their composition, giving them a very romantic style.

Small and Large English Museum

In July of 1989 I returned to London, England where my son lives and works. Because of my personal interest, we intended to continue visiting museums which had collections of *samplers*. After a week Gulia met me and we proceeded enthusiastically with our research. We visited many museums besides the ones which I will discuss here and we were always greeted with the utmost courtesy. One must keep in mind that most embroidery pieces are not placed on display and therefore, to see them, the director would need to assign us a guide to assist us. We were often convinced that these people found pleasure in allowing us to be part of the beauty which they preserved. We were never under the impression that the various samplers, even the most valuable ones, were considered sole property of the director.

Visiting these museums "behind the scenes," as we were able to do, is definitely an interesting and unusual experience. The possibility of admiring the objects in a different atmosphere than that of the usual exhibit and being able to carefully touch and turn them over, renders the objects far more personal. It is fascinating to see a woman wearing an apron and rubber

Sampler embroidered in cross stitch with silk thread on linen fabric, 21" x 22-1/2". Netherlands, 1842. Typical motifs of the Dutch production are the stylized masculine figures and the vase with a bunch of flowers. Florence, Palazzo Davanzati.

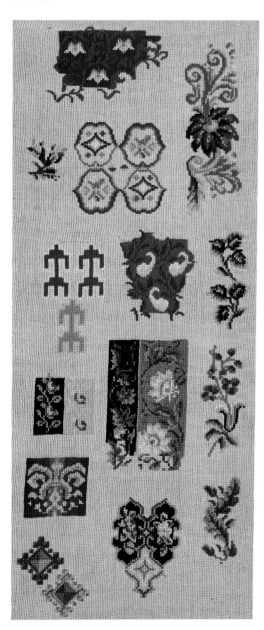

Sampler embroidered in wool on etamine. London. Victoria and Albert Museum.

gloves, dusting rare and precious objects, during closing hours or a man relocating famous paintings, putting them to one side to await their move to another exhibit.

In various museums we found quite a bit of interesting material. In others, we were not able to find samples of interest to us even though they had many beautiful pieces. I would like to indicate certain particularly unusual museums, apart from any embroidery collection, that are probably less frequented. One is the American Museum of Bath located in the Claverton Manor residence which I will cover later.

London, Victoria and Albert Museum

What is there left to say that has not already been said about this universally recognized museum? It was founded in 1852 as the "museum of handmade articles" to help students in their studies, apprentices of artisans, and students of the academies that were dedicated to design and painting. In 1899 Queen Victoria bestowed upon the museum the name of her spouse, Prince Albert, in whose memory it was dedicated. The museum, which today is one of the largest and most important in the world, actually contains many museums in one: nine departments have developed in an area covering 650,000 square feet with a collection of many precious objects.

In various rooms, perfect recreations of historical settings have been brought to life, with special attention to every detail. Entire departments have been dedicated to

Facing page, sampler exceptionally full of motifs, embroidered in silk on linen, beautiful in the composition and very refined in the choice of colors. It is signed by the authoress, Elizabeth S. Musto, only fourteen years old. London, Victoria and Albert Museum.

THE REQUEST

Father whate'er of earthly bliss,
Thy sovreign will denies,
Accepted at thy throne of grace,
Let this petition rise.

Give me a calm a thankful heart,
From every murmur free,
The blessings of thy grace impart,
And make me live to thee.

Elizabeth S Multo
Her Work
Aged 14 Years.

musical instruments, clothing, embroidery, miniatures, paintings, and sculptures to name a few of the decorative arts.

Naturally, Gulia and I spent the majority of our time in the section of textile arts, where the extensive collection of samplers can be found. Among the various types of embroidery displayed, the samplers are the most numerous: this is easily explained by recalling that from the early seventeenth to the first decade of the twentieth century, children and adolescents created many embroidered pieces during school lessons. The oldest examples, of which few have survived, date back to 1502. There are two other samplers in the museum that even though undated, may be attributed to the sixteenth century: one, perhaps German, captures figurative themes of sacred subjects along with decorative motifs of an exquisitely decorative character. The other, definitely Italian, is full of ornamental motifs.

More numerous are the pieces which may be dated to the seventeenth century; they are recognizable by their long and narrow form (from 6 to 12 inches high and from 12 to 60 inches long) and by the vividness and brightness of the colors of the decorative motifs, often inspired by nature: flowers,

Sampler with various types of embroidery done in cross stitch on linen. XIXth century. London, Victoria and Albert Museum.

birds and fish. Certain *samplers* are embroidered entirely in silk, others in linen but most often varying types of threads are intertwined with only the borders in silk.

During the eighteenth century squarer canvases were substituted for the long ones; the inscriptions were more frequent, more or less long and complex, very often ingenious, and at times with authentic poetic accents. The decorative motifs tended to become more pictorial and were enclosed within very rich borders.

During the first half of the nineteenth century styles and trends of the previous century were maintained, containing few variations with respect to that tradition. The major innovation seems to be the tendency to give relief to the figures with skillful shading, in contrast to the very two-dimensional motifs and stylized forms of the preceding century. Undoubtedly, in order to achieve this complexity, the dissemination of hand-made embroidery patterns was critical. The embroiderers could now reproduce even the most complex subjects.

During the second half of the nineteenth century however, the *sampler* became partially free of its function as a subordinate element of women's education, whose composition was very rigid, complying with traditional and scholastic decorative themes. Due to the great enthusiasm and inspiration of various amateurs, the themes became more liberated in the choice of subjects and colors, achieving results of great enlightenment and esthetic gracefulness, even though a beginner's work was not always a work of art. Among such an abundance of pieces it was not easy to choose but I am certain the samplers which I selected have not only the richest decorative themes but are also the most significant of the age to which I have dedicated my research.

London, Bethnal Green Museum

Bethnal Green is the most important toy museum in all of England and it represents a branch of the Victoria and Albert Museum.

The small *souvenir-guide* it states: «The Victoria and Albert is devoted to beautiful and useful objects created by man and the museum of Bethnal Green to those created for their children. Following the art of design and the reproduction of toys throughout history one learns that every generation repeats the same things but they are altered and further developed. That which the child sees in the old toys of Bethnal Green will help him when he is grown, to appreciate the works of art of the Victoria and Albert Museum».

Footstool for a child embroidered with wool in petit point. XIXth century. London, Bethnal Green Museum.

I find this observation very interesting and worthy of greater deliberation. Other than possessing the richest existing collection of toys, the Bethnal Green Museum contains a collection of children's clothes from the eighteenth century to the present day, typically complemented by stunning accessories: hats, stockings, purses and shoes. The children's clothing is embellished with embroidery and lace and a pair of satin slippers, which immediately capturied ately capturied my attention, was embroidered with small cross-stitch. The museum also conserves a lovely small footstool for children, embroidered in petit point. Another exhibit is dedicated to needlepoint, among which there are various samplers, and to students notebooks containing sewn and embroidered exercises.

Bath, Claverton Manor, American Museum in Britain

The American Museum is situated in Claverton Manor, a splendid country residence in the county of Avon, about two miles from the eighteenth century city of Bath. The building, situated in a prominent location facing the valley where the Avon River flows, was designed in 1820 by Sir Jeffry Wyatville, architect of George IV. Here Winston Churchill held his first political discussion on July 26, 1897.

The first American Museum in a foreign country, it was founded by two Americans, Dallas Pratte and John Judkyn. Fond of the art of their native land, they were eager to spread the study of American culture and history to the rest of the world. The museum was inaugurated July 1st, 1961.

The objects collected represent the period of time between the late seventeenth century and mid twentieth century. In this collection the examples representing Puritan English culture are mixed with Spanish examples. Each setting illustrates a region and historical period.

One Monday morning Gulia and I visited Bath, where we were greeted by the lovely Mrs. Shelag Ford. The road that runs from the center of Bath to the museum is particularly scenic, rich in greenery, as it merges gracefully with the surrounding hills. That day the museum was closed to the public, making our visit quite pleasant. Mrs. Ford received us amiably and was a considerate hostess. The presence of maids tidying up gave the interior a lived-in appearance, rendering the visit informal and giving us the feeling of not being in a

Small shoe for a child embroidered in petit point in silk on white linen. XIX century. London, Bethnal Green Museum.

The Prince of peace is come;
Ye nations should and sing.
Let men and angels Join their songs,
To hail this glorious King.

Hannah Leiss, my affectionale Aunt &
Patroness.

Sampler embroidered in cross stitch and petit point on very fine linen, signed and dated by the authoress, Rebecca van Gresemer. England, 1835. Bath, Claverton Manor, American Museum in Britain.

museum. The atmosphere at Claverton Manor is not in the least bit solemn and gives one impression of wandering through an elegant, upper-class country home. The different rooms with their furnishings, wainscots and the floors, which were imported from the United States, are originally from different places and different centuries, and offer an unusual journey. The first pioneers, arriving in the New World with their baggage of culture and traditions were obligated to reinterpret this heritage through innovation: using different materials and supplementing it with their imagination, encouraging artistic expression, vital and full of originality. The museum conserves beautiful pieces of silver, glass, fabrics and precious objects from everyday use.

The section dedicated to textiles holds a rich collection of pieces from the eighteenth and nineteenth centuries: quilts, patchwork, hand-woven towels, and *samplers* created by the first colonists. The pieces which interested us weren't many so I chose only one. However, it is such a beautiful place that I do not regret the time spent at this interesting museum. Among the more interesting things we recall is the still functional American country kitchen, the "Colonial Herb Garden," and the "Mount Vernon Garden." The former garden contains diverse species of imported colonial herbs and those introduced by the Indians. These were used for cooking and making decorations and medicines. The latter is a small reproduction of the garden that surrounded George Washington's home in Virginia.

Cambridge, The Fitzwilliam Museum

Small purse embroidered in silk and silver threads. XVIIth century. Cambridge, Fitzwilliam Museum.

The Fitzwilliam Museum, one of the most important English museums of figurative and applied arts, originated from the donated collections of the Viscount Fitzwilliam to the University of Cambridge in 1816.

It wasn't possible for me to visit the entire museum because, even though I had an appointment with the director of the textile department to examine the famous *samplers,* that

Sampler in salmon colored linen with a rich and precious floral border in cross stitch that enclose samples of the more common types of domestic mending. England, 1843. Cambridge, Fitzwilliam Museum.

person wasn't present the day of our visit and the embroidery rooms were closed to the public. Seeing that we were quite disappointed, a timid, polite woman was able to find the key to some of the rooms and showed us around. Therefore the research of this collection was done in part from direct experience and in part from the catalogue of the museum.

The samplers from the Fitzwilliam museum are for the most part from two different important donations: one from

Doctor J.W.L. Glaisher in 1928 and the other from Mrs. H.A. Longman in 1938. Nearly thirty pieces conserved in the museum are antique and are in excellent condition. One hundred and eleven are from the seventeenth century, one hundred and twenty from the eighteenth century and fifty-seven from the nineteenth century. The display has less than one hundred pieces (the others are in storage), organized chronologically and each century is divided into categories depending on their type and quality. This type of organization helps the visitor see the evolution of a technique and style through the passage of time. It also shows the continuation and affinity in those four centuries for a type of work that had profound roots and motivations in tradition.

Edinburgh, The Royal Scottish Museum

The collection of samplers conserved in this museum consists of one hundred and two pieces. It is not a vast collection but is very representative of the entire story of samplers from many of the countries that produced this type of work. There are no examples of American, Italian or Scandinavian embroidery but there are some very old pieces.

Obviously the majority of the pieces are Scottish and they don't differ much from those that were done in other parts of Great Britain except for the frequency with which the names and initials of the young embroideresses are present.

Although I was not able to see the entire collection

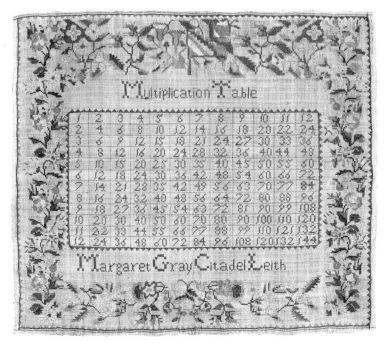

Sampler in cross stitch in silk on wool; 32,5x38 cm. It is embroidered with the multiplication table enclosed by a floral border and signed by the authoress, Margaret Gray. She also indicates the place that it was done, the ruins of the Citadel Leith, near Edinburgh, where during the XIXth century there were many artisan workshops. England, 1820-40. Edinburgh, The Royal Scottish Museum.

of *samplers,* because not all were on exhibit, I was able to examine ten pieces which an employee graciously removed from storage. I then completed my knowledge of the collection studying the exceptional catalog.

All the embroidered patterns conserved in the Royal Scottish Museum are filed and organized chronologically and by town of origin. The dimensions, date of creation, prevalent colors, type of stitching, type and quality of threads and the material used for the background are indicated for each piece.

Embroidery in silk on linen, 70x75 cm, with the central scene of watering deer enclosed by a series of rich and elaborate borders. England, about 1850. Edinburgh, The Royal Scottish Museum.

There are about eighty British works (dating from 1650 to 1939), three Bulgarian patterns (from 1946), two French (from mid nineteenth century), three German and four Mexican (from the nineteenth century), and two Spanish (one dated 1750, the other 1850). Lastly, there is a Swiss sample and an American one, both recent, and an Indian example from the early twentieth century made in Calcutta entirely in silk on cotton material.

In my opinion, the most beautiful embroidery is a piece dating back to the middle of the nineteenth century. It is very large (28 x 30 inches), containing splendid scenery with deer which is surrounded by a very wide, elaborate border between more simple borders of colorful flowers that enclose the composition.

A Private Visit in Germany

My research continued in the fall of the same year in Germany. We wanted a documentary on German *samplers*, to obtain a sense of the famous *Berlin wool work* and the wool embroidery of Berlin, very widespread in the nineteenth century.

Much of the material had been lost during the war, even though a large quantity remains. Despite the extensive collection, one has the impression that in Germany today few pursue this national heritage of cross stitch and petit point. Few stores sell kits, and these are usually very simple and uninteresting, and there is little literature in the libraries to stimulate interest. It is a situation, therefore, different from the English one where the tradition of *samplers* is still very much alive and the literature very extensive.

The city of Essen was our first stop on this trip. We were welcomed by Mrs. Ursula Joka-Deubelius, whom we had already met at Colonia two years before while visiting an embroidery exhibit. An ex-financial journalist, she decided at one point during her life to deal with embroidery as a collector and then as a producer of kits. Her home was full of embroidery, samples and designs that left us in awe and speechless. She was full of advice and suggestions, helping us with our museum visits with which we had made reservations.

I like recalling the night spent in the apartment where Frau Joka works and where she welcomed us as her guests: three ample rooms simply and traditionally furnished in sweet-smelling, natural wood. There were books, article clippings, designs, fabrics and all the materials needed to create the kits. We slept in the room reserved for thread preparation. On an enormous table, divided in sections, were hundreds of spools of threads of all colors while one wall was entirely covered with shelves full of bobbins, likewise holding threads of all shades and gradations.

Celle, Das Deutsche Stickmuster Museum

Sampler embroidered in cross stitch in wool on etamine, 39x56 cm, initialed and dated by the authoress. Switzerland, 1868. Celle, Das Deutsche Stickmuster Museum.

From Essen we proceeded towards Hamburg to find Buxtehude where the Stickmuster Museum was located, about 30 miles from the center of the city. When we arrived we found ourselves in front of a small villa, a private residence, where we were greeted by Elfi and Hans Joachim Connemann. The Connemann couple are passionate collectors of valuable *samplers* and have established an entire museum in their home, reserving the first floor for exhibitions. It is a small but well utilized space. On the bare walls framed *samplers* are hung and below, on a series of white shelves which run along the perimeter of the walls, are books and magazines on embroidery from all over the world. In the center, glass cases enclose displays of small objects: jewelry boxes, purses, picture frames, and wallets many of which are embroidered in petit point with glass beads, or in silk on velvet. One can also appreciate the embroidery kits complete with scissors, needles, thimbles, and all the necessary materials to create works of art.

Above, detail from a sampler embroidered in silk on linen with a family scene on a background of a flowering garden in a typical romantic style. Denmark, 1846. Celle, Das Deutsche Stickmuster Museum.

The pleasantness of our hosts was equal to that of the environment in which they lived. The warm, cozy home contained a gorgeous loom which stood out among the rest of the furniture on which Mrs. Elfi was in the process of weaving a beautiful pattern. In the fall of 1990 the Connemanns transferred their museum to Celle, near Hannover. About 3,000 pieces from the collection are displayed in a Rococo palace built in 1770 for Prince Ernesto of Maklemblurg-Strelitz, presently the headquarters of the Civic Archives.

Hamburg, Museum fur Kunst und Gewerbe

The Museum fur Kunst und Gewerbe, dedicated to the decorative arts, is in a palace built in 1877. It contains ninety-nine rooms, with exhibits of European decorative art from

Detail of a sampler embroidered in cross stitch in silk on linen with a border of leaves, flowers and fruit. 1837. Hamburg, Museum fur Kunst und Gewerbe.

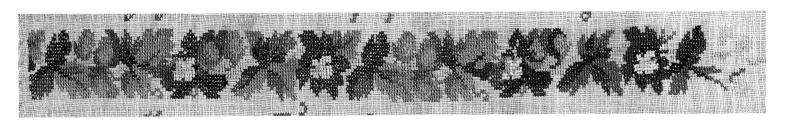

the Byzantine Era to the present day. Pieces of Romanesque art, an important collection of Limoges enamel, Italian art, a precious collection of Renaissance bronze pieces, Gothic tapestries of Flemish creation, sixteenth century Italian majolica, and a splendid collection of German Renaissance ceramics make up the principal subjects preserved in this rich museum. Among the many collections there are about 25,000 textile pieces, 70% of which can be attributed to the work of collector Justus Brinkmann, the museum director for many years.

His large spectrum of interests was reflected in the diversity of his collections: oriental rugs, tapestries from the eighteenth century to the present; Coptic, Byzantine, Islamic, Oriental, and Middle-eastern fabrics; European fabrics of every era; Eastern European and Asian embroidery, costumes and accessories from the eighteenth century to the present; liturgical vestments; Asiatic and rural costumes; and house linens and textiles used for furnishings. Since 1975 these collections have been preserved in storerooms of the

On this page two samplers embroidered in cross stitch on linen, the one on the left from 1832 and on the right from 1841. Hamburg, Museum für Kunst und Gewerbe.

Detail of a basket of flowers from a sampler, embroidered in cross stitch with silk on white linen. 1817. Hamburg, Museum für Kunst und Gewerbe.

museum. The textile collection is attached to the textile restoration workshop that is also used as a school. The collection of nearly 600 embroidery pieces is absolutely unique. We were greeted by Mrs. Ursula Strate who accompanied us through a tour of impressive stairs and corridors to an enormous, illuminated showroom where the extensive collection of *samplers* and embroidered objects was housed. We were given much freedom and time to examine the pieces carefully, with the director present to help us when needed.

The room was furnished with large antique armoires containing drawers in which the embroideries were stored. On enormous tables lay antique clothes, hats, and gloves, ready to be restored or already restored, wrapped in tissue paper.

Altona, Hamburg, Altonaer Museum

The Altonaer Museum is primarily dedicated to natural history and the ethnography of the region. Besides prehistoric findings, ships, utensils, models and the creation of rural settings, ceramics, fabrics, and toys, the museum also contains a collection of *samplers* that are generally not exhibited to the public. The director, Mrs. Gisela Soltkahn, was absent, but she kindly saw to it that we had access to all the necessary materials from the workshop of the museum. After having examined the material

Detail of a basket of fruit from an embroidered sampler in cross stitch on linen. Altona, Hamburg, Altonaer Museum.

we departed for Berlin.

Berlin, Kunstbibliothek

Just as in Hamburg, we made use of the library in Berlin, accompanied by the soft whisper of the linen maid: "Two Italian writers!" The director, Mrs. Gretel Wagner, came to greet us, accompanied by two assistants. They had already prepared on a table some of the oldest and most precious volumes on whose pages were faded patterns of cross stitch, scribbled in red ink. Even appreciating the historical importance, we froze at the sight of the imperial-looking eagles created with small red dots. Many other books and loose designs were shown to us and when we finally identified a colored design typical of the period we were interested in, it was clear, even to our hosts, what we were looking for. Having pinpointed the theme which was most important to us, the director lead us to the upper level of the library where we were given an enormous box, the first in a series of eight. When we removed the cover, we were awestruck and surprised to find hundreds of tempera and water color designs on blue graph paper: they were the famous patters of *Berlin wool work*. It would take many days to examine the contents of the boxes. The subjects that flashed before our eyes, as we handled the patterns with the utmost care, were extremely varied and all very beautiful. There were designs dedicated to children and to children's games, often with animals participating, on a background of innocent and simple scenery and small hunting scenes with proud hunters, accompanied by the typical dog, who aim at prey while hiding among finely outlined bushes. The rich borders are of diverse importance and dimensions, from the smallest, one half inch high, to ones eight to twelve inches made for rugs, with complex floral designs, braided ribbons and the traditional decorative repertoire

Facing page, sampler embroidered with cross stitch on linen with a rich and varied sample of designs. Initialed and dated. 1843. Altona. Hamburg. Altonaer Museum.

Detail from a sampler embroidered in cross stitch on linen. 1817. Hamburg. Museum für Kunst und Gewerbe.

reinterpreted with vivacity and fresh color. There are patterns for draperies, pillows, foot stools, and small rugs; big and small garlands, thin or full, bouquets of flowers and splendid colorful baskets.

There are patterns for tea cozies with the typical semicircular form, with minute subjects, funny and gracious animals, patterns for embroidering purses with glass beads or petit point, and hundreds of patterns for creating embroidered slippers for men, women, and children.

Nine months later, with permission from the director, Professor Evers, I returned to Berlin to choose the graphic material for this book. Even on this second visit to Kunstbibliothek, I felt great emotion seeing those designs again. To make a reasonable choice among the diverse subjects, I carefully re-examined all the material. The selection was not easy because they were all worthy of being published.

Assisted by the attentive Doctor Christina Thon and by the patient Mr. Mayer, I worked in absolute tranquillity for three days in a room reserved for me.

The patterns for what will be called *Berlin wool work* came to light in Berlin at the beginning of the nineteenth century. It was in 1804 that an editor in Berlin got the idea to publish patterns for embroidery printed on graph paper. The great novelty was that they were offered in color, and due to their precision and clarity, they could be copied if one had the patience to follow the design. In fact, every little square on the paper corresponded to a stitch; *petit point*, half stitch, or cross stitch, which would be worked on an even weave fabric. Many editors and printers followed the example and the "Embroidery of Berlin" became, in Europe, the most popular form of embroidery. The designs, previously sketched by hand, as well as the squares and borders, were transferred onto copper plates for printing. On the printed sheet the color was created by hand with water colors and tempera. Later, the same designs were printed and painted directly onto the canvas. Today this method is still used although in my experience, I can confirm that in order to create a perfect pattern, it is preferable to follow a design on paper. To create a perfect embroidery it was necessary to obtain a perfect fabric; a fabric with an even weave in both directions like the canvas called *Penelope* cloth, which is still used for half stitch and cross stitch. Other fabrics were used as well, such as linen, wool, and silk. The silk fabric has a very thin weft on which the work acquires a marvelous finish and allows the possibility of not having to embroider the entire canvas.

Wool or silk threads were used, both often intertwined in the same work, the silk giving the design luminosity and delicacy. In Berlin, in the nineteenth century, a special wool for embroidering was produced. It was soft and light and most important, had an uniform structure. The range of colors must have been quite vast as we can deduce from the surviving pieces which are rich in tones, shades, and hues.

Detail from a sampler embroidered in cross stitch with wool on etamine. Celle, Das Deutsche Stickmuster Museum.

These threads had the advantage of not succumbing to changes, such as the discoloration from light. For this reason, the work created in the early nineteenth century is well preserved and the colors, despite the exposure to sunlight and dust, vary only slightly with the colors on the reverse side. In the second half of the century, Sir William Perkins discovered the aniline colors which soon invaded the European market. These are industrially produced and used to dye threads in an infinite range of colors.

It is very difficult today to imagine the extent of this style of embroidery. One only needs to think that the word "embroidery" for a period of time, meant only the *Berlin wool work*, a particular "genre" that seemed to absorb in itself every other type of needlework. As Molly G. Proctor explains in *Victorian Canvas*, the great success of the "Embroidery of Berlin" was that it was favored by the Industrial Revolution, which at one point favored the formation and expansion of a bourgeois class as well as the improvement of the lower class. This new and larger "feminine" middle class, formed by the wives of entrepreneurs or proprietors with the newly acquired wealth, were eased from their domestic chores if not from hard agricultural labor. They finally had the time to dedicate themselves to literature, music, paintings and of course, embroidery. Most of all, the latter, easily transportable, became an inseparable companion of women. During afternoon tea-time or during evening meetings in the dining room, the women conversed with their guests and family members while attending to their *needlepoint*. No woman could escape the fascination of this work, not even queens.

I would like to point out that a similar phenomenon, more relevant in numerical terms, has exploded in recent years. The 60s, 70s and 80s of this century sees a decrease in births, diffusion of electrical appliances, frozen and pre-cooked foods, and the new norm for women -- the work day away from home for specific times. These "liberated" women, with few children and much help from modern technology, even though occupied in activities outside of the home, find time to dedicate to sports, shows and relaxation; in other words, to themselves. In this new way of life, there is probably even time to spare for a renewed interest in needlepoint: an activity in which the pleasure of relaxation mixes with expressions that evoke distant yet familiar

Detail from a sampler of a vase and a rose branch, embroidered in cross stitch in silk on a dense woven linen. Italy, first half of the XIXth century. Florence, Palazzo Davanzati.

Detail from a sampler of a vase and a lily branch, embroidered in cross stitch in silk on a dense woven linen. Italy, first half of the XIXth century. Florence, Palazzo Davanzati.

situations. They bring to mind pleasurable fantasies and tranquil atmospheres free of melancholy. Now, much like before, the embroiderer is enriched by the joy and the self-realization that only creative work can bring: work that is generated by one's own hands, with precision, pleasure and sensitivity.

This is the first time that I am writing something which is not a letter to a friend. Among my many interests, writing is not one of them and neither is poetry, novels or keeping diaries. Therefore, I do not know how successful I am in communicating my enthusiasm to others.

In choosing the illustrations for this book, the criteria is that they are of significance not only to those who have cultural interests but to those simply moved by the desire to recreate these illustrated subjects through embroidery.

Detail from a sampler embroidered in cross stitch on linen. 1832. Hamburg. Museum für Kunst und Gewerbe.

PATTERNS
FOR
BERLIN WOOL WORK

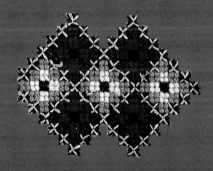

Floral Compositions

"Requiem" of the Rose

*«A rose was dying. She slowly stooped upon her stem
and her corolla gradually turned pale. The bees and butterflies
had tried in vain to revive her with the soft caresses
of their gilded wings; white lilies also reached to
give their dewdrops that shone with the rays
of the sun like iridescent pearls; and in vain
the wind had tried to gently blow her stem straight...
But it was all in vain, as the rose faded towards her death...
It was the first rose of the year that had gone in that sad way
and they all whispered among themselves
that they also would leave as she had,
quaking with the thought of it...
And with the evening moonlight, whose glimmering rays
glowed off the silvery wings of bugs and the sensuous folds of flowers,
a slow procession stirred to bury one of their own.
The solemn lilies led, while the carnations dressed in red velvet
followed in succession with the field poppies not far behind...
Then came a long white flow of daisies and
spring flowers with violets in their clothes of mourning...
The other flowers arrived between the wings of grasshoppers,
armed with long threads of grass, on
silently suffering butterflies, tit mice,*

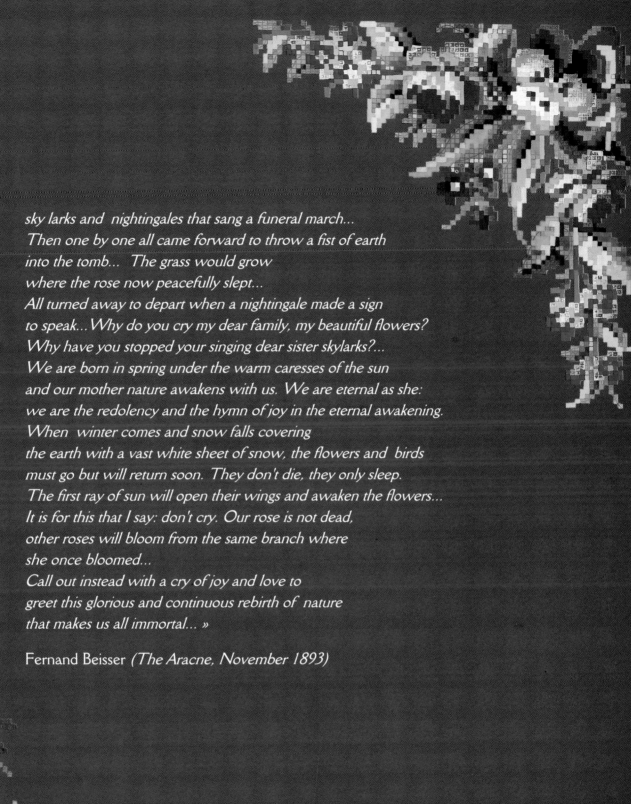

sky larks and nightingales that sang a funeral march...
Then one by one all came forward to throw a fist of earth
into the tomb...   The grass would grow
where the rose now peacefully slept...
All turned away to depart when a nightingale made a sign
to speak...Why do you cry my dear family, my beautiful flowers?
Why have you stopped your singing dear sister skylarks?...
We are born in spring under the warm caresses of the sun
and our mother nature awakens with us. We are eternal as she:
we are the redolency and the hymn of joy in the eternal awakening.
When winter comes and snow falls covering
the earth with a vast white sheet of snow, the flowers and birds
must go but will return soon. They don't die, they only sleep.
The first ray of sun will open their wings and awaken the flowers...
It is for this that I say: don't cry. Our rose is not dead,
other roses will bloom from the same branch where
she once bloomed...
Call out instead with a cry of joy and love to
greet this glorious and continuous rebirth of nature
that makes us all immortal... »

Fernand Beisser *(The Aracne, November 1893)*

Among the more frequent subject models for *Berlin wool work* are certainly floral designs: in the form of baskets, bunches, vine shoots or festoons, as well as in the use of simple buds for small and delicate details. The rich range of hues, that allows for an overall flowing image in the realization of the embroidery, gives these tempera or watercolor sketches the brightness of a beautifully composed painting. .

FESTOON OF ROSES

Rose
Violet Pink	■	3328
Dark Pink	▽	760
Pink	::	761
Pale Pink	C	948
White Pink	.	3770
Dark Rosy Beige	◐	758
Pale Rosy Beige	\	945
White Rosy Beige	ɯ	951
Ecru	I	712

Leaves and Stems
Dark Green	●	934
Dark Moss Green	U	3051
Pale Moss Green	\	3053
Peacock Green	∟	501
Pale Peacock Green	V	502
Palest Green	S	503
Yellow Green	□	3013
Ivory	I	712

The finished embroidery is a part of the sampler illustrated on page 73.

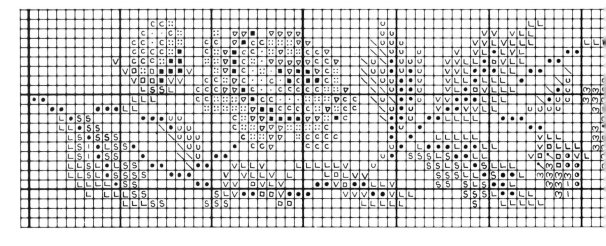

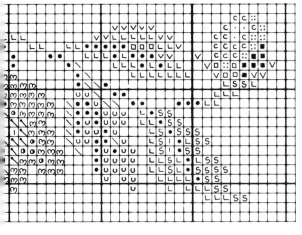

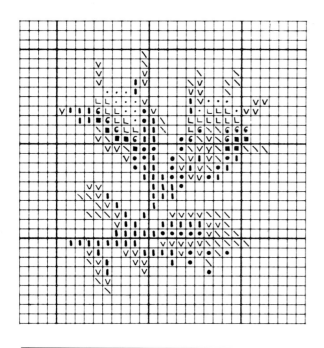

ROSE BUD

Leaves			Rose		
Black	●	310	Red	■	326
Dark Green	I	934	Pink	𝄢	335
Green	∪	936	White Pink	L	776
Yellow Green	▽	581	White	·	819
Pale Yellow	╱	472			

This embroidery is a part of the sampler illustrated on page 72.

SMALL TEMPLE

Trees

Pale Yellow Green	C	733
Dark Yellow Green	╲	732
Pale Green	L	936
Dark Green	I	934
Brown	■	433

Earth

Black Brown	●	3371
Dark Brown	○	801
Dark Green	I	934
Pale Green	L	936
Pale Yellow Green	C	733
Dark Yellow Green	╲	732
Ochre	□	435

Sanctuary

Dark Gray	▲	535
Gray	▽	318
Pale Gray	╱	762
Chestnut-brown	×	839
Brown	╲	433
Ochre	◑	435
Beige	·	738
Yellow	㎜	725
Black Violet	◣	791
Dark Violet	Ψ	333
Violet	P	209
Pale Violet	I	211

The embroidery is a part of the sampler illustrated on page 84.

4201.

ROSE

Leaves

Dark Green	**I**	934
Peacock Green	△	500
Pale Peacock Green	V	501
Warm Green	U	520
Warm Pale Green	L	522
Pale Yellow	○	3053

Branch

Dark Brown	■	869
Pale Brown	□	370

Rose

Violet Pink	●	3778
Dark Pink	'	758
Pink	×	945
Pale Pink	/	951
White Pink	.	712

The embroidery is a part of the sampler shown on page 73.

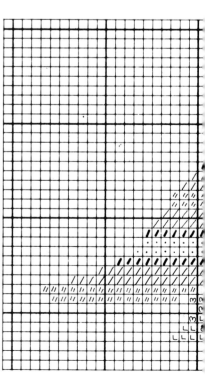

ROSES AND RIBBON

Ribbon			Leaves			Pink Rose		
Dark Blue	╱	939	Black Green	▼	500	Dark Red	●	814
Blue	╱	930	Dark Green	⦶	3345	Red	◑	326
Sky-Blue	∥	931	Green	∟	3346	Pink	▽	899
Light Blue	.	775	Pale Yellow	ɯ	3348	Pale Pink	::	776
Dark Brown	■	898				White	I	819
Brown	□	434	**Red Rose**					
Beige	V	738	Dark Red	●	814			
			Red	I	304	*The embroidery is a part*		
			Orange	○	349	*of the sampler* illustrated		
			Dark Pink	⋏	352	*on page 74.*		

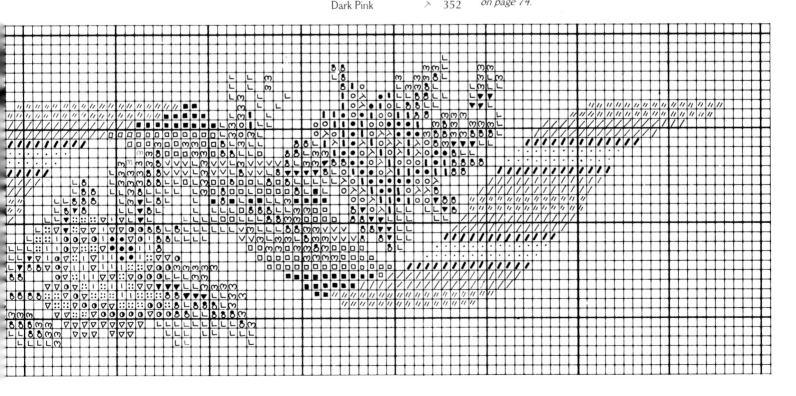

FESTOON

First Flower

Dark Pink	◑	223
Pale Pink	○	224
Bordeaux	∟	3350

Branch

Rust Brown	×	433

Foliage

Dark Green	I	935
Pale Green	∪	3362

Second Flower

Dark Vivid Pink	::	962
Pale Vivid Pink	◺	3689
Bordeaux	∟	3350

The embroidery is shown on page 5.

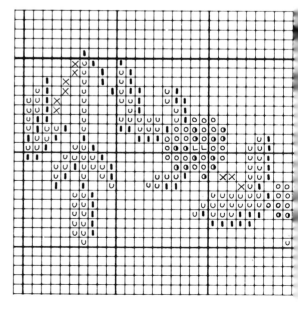

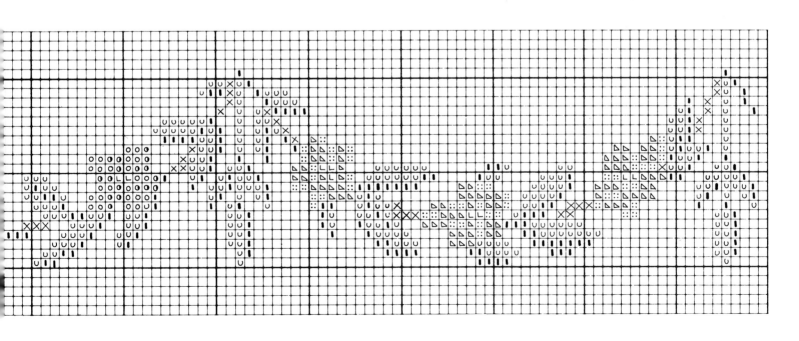

BASKET OF FLOWERS

Meadow			Basket			Pale flowers		
Dark Green	●	500	Brown	✔	869	Pink	ٔ	758
Green	∟	501	White Brown	△	3045	Pale Pink	//	950
Pale Green	∣	502	Beige	V	3047	Ecru	ɯ	3770
			White Beige	.	746			
Leaves						**Flowers on top**		
Dark Green	●	500	**Dark flowers**			Blue	∣	930
Green	∟	501	Dark Pink	■	356	Pale Blue	C	932
White Green	∪	503	Pink	☐	3064	Sky-Blue	○	928
Yellow Green	＼	3869	Pale Pink	//	950	Pale Pink	//	950
			Beige	Z	739	White Pink	ɯ	3770

The embroidery is a part of the sampler illustrated on page 73

108

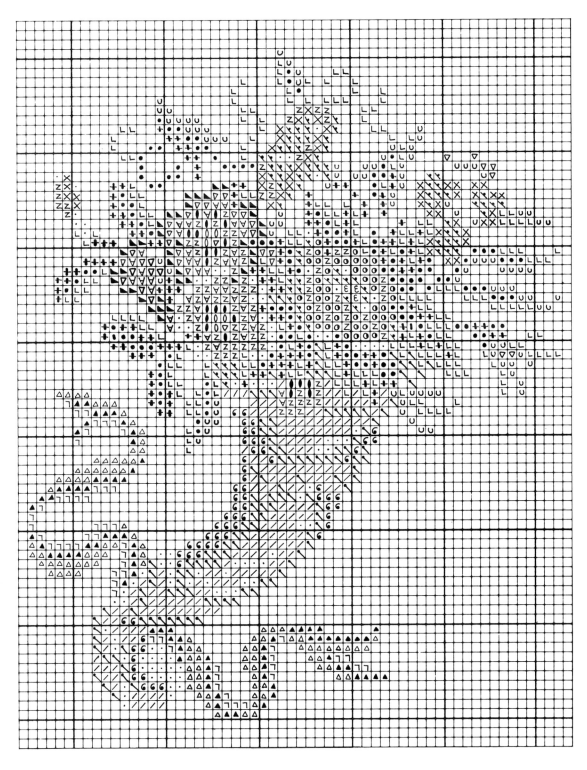

CORNUCOPIA

Leaves

Dark Moss Green	●	934
Dark Green	+	501
Green	L	502
Pale Green	U	504

Cornucopia

Dark Hazelnut	⸸	435
Hazelnut	\	437
Ecru	/	738
White	.	739

Flowers

Rosy Beige	◑	758
Beige	Z	754
White Pink	✴	3770
Dark Orange	◀	976
Pale Orange	▽	729
Gray Green	◖	524
Brown Green	0	610
Gray Violet	∀	370
Gray	×	3013

Ribbon

Dark Pink	⌐	3778
Pale Pink	△	3779
Blue	▲	930

The embroidery is part of the sampler shown on page 73.

Violets

*«The city is full of them and even those that have decided to spend
only a penny from their own expenses for some poetry, can carry
for the day a small bunch of these flowers with their famous sweet
perfume... no one can resist the sweet fascination of a bunch of
violets...Doesn't it seem that violets have a perfume of the past
that makes them especially attractive, even to those that are able to
look back with distance, not feeling the past's melancholic
tugs on the heart?...
The violet is a personal flower, linked to an individual; they
don't like to show themselves on a table in a big
bunch of flashy flowers or on stuffy over done cushions; they are
a flower that has a need of intimacy...
...And don't give away the violets that come from people that you
love, or that you have once loved, or that love you; other flowers
may be empty, they could be the gift from just anyone, but not
the small violets, tender yet passionate».*

(The Aracne, February 1894)

The models for the *Berlin wool work* were published for the first time in Berlin in 1804 by the German publisher Philisson, who had the idea of putting the embroidery designs on checkered paper: each small square on the paper corresponding to a stitch - *petit-point*, half stitch or cross stitch - making it possible to copy with extreme precision any design.

Crowns and Wreathes

«The legend attributes the creation of the crown to Giano
Bifronte. Arguing from the silence of Homer it seems
that in the heroic era the crown was not yet used amongst the
Greek as a festive ornament, a reward, or as a sign of dignity;
but in a hymn to Venus the goddess comes described
with a golden crown on her head...
The crown of Jupiter, for example, was of various flowers;
Hercules' was made of poplar; Apollo's of laurel; vine leaves and
grape clusters that of Bacchus; while Venus wore the fair cap of
myrtle and roses, Minerva had olives, Ceres wore ears of corn,
and that of Numis was made of reed leaves... With the birth of a
boy in Rome and Athens a garland of ivy or olives
was hung in the entrance of the house. In Greece and later
also in Rome garlands of myrtle and of roses were placed on
the wedding bed and the newlyweds were adorned with crowns...
If so much dignity was given to wreathes and crowns for the dead,
we must wonder about how much
this ornament was liked by the living.
The women wove them in the
intimacy of their gynaeceum and
the freshest aether was always
kept in their home for friends...
Bald people believed that a
crown, especially made of
vine leaves, replaced a wig
and therefore there were
no more elderly people or at
least that the damages and
wrinkles of old age were not
the first thing seen... In France,
the first of the European countries
that was legally formed under the
dominion of a king, the regal crowns
went through various modifications
in the passing of centuries.

Under Louis XIVth crowns fell into disuse
because of the enormous wigs
that were then in fashion...they
would have been aesthetically
out of proportion. Face powder
was the cause for which the
ladies of the XVIIIth century
abandoned the crowns of
gold and pearls for garlands
of flowers that not only
attractively adorned their
graceful heads, but could also
almost protect their modesty,
flowing down their white shoulders
and descending in lovely festoons
to complement the fresh breeziness
of their Watteau muslin clothes. But if
fashion banned women from using crowns,
the custom of the use of crowns as prizes remained...
Those who should never have stopped wearing the simple and
poetic ornamentation of flower garlands, which was the custom in
the times of Grillandaio, were the women. On their young heads of
hair, brown or blonde, the garlands certainly looked better than hats.
However the young girls of Cofte adorned their heads with fresh
flowers, as did the Italic young girls in the time of Beatrice; now an
artful flower, a butterfly or a ribbon...suffices for this decoration...as
long as they are not yet sixteen years old...when they begin to want a
crown of orange flowers. The only wish of the daily prose is that it
hasn't lost its poetic meaning...which is what I wish from my heart
to all my young readers».

Maria Bobba *(The Aracne, May 1893)*

The place of honor, among the selected flowers for the "Berlin embroideries", is certainly given to the rose that appears in most of these delicate sketches. Special attention is also granted to violets, a flower very much in harmony with the taste and sensibility of the nineteenth century. Also very frequent are the hawthorn, poppy, tulip, daisy, thrush and forget-me-not.

GARLAND

Black Green	●	500		⩔	209
Dark Green	Q	319	Violet	Y	211
Green	U	988	Pale Violet	P	318
Pale Green	+	3347	Dark Gray	✚	415
Greenish	L	3348	Pale Gray	.	Neige
Dark Red	◖	902	White	⊙	433
Magenta	■	815	Light Brown	Ɐ	834
Shiny Red	V	817	Yellow Gold	⑪	518
Pink	∷	335	Turquoise	◐	824
Pale Pink	‖	3326	Light Blue	Z	3766
White Pink	\	818	Light Blue		
Orange	▲	350			
Yellow	△	676	*This garland is embroidered*		
Ochre	S	680	*in the center purse shown on*		
Dark Violet	⬥	550	*page 66.*		

The original models for *Berlin wool work* were engraved on copper, printed, and then colored with tempera or water colors. This lightly tinted paper always had a type of frame, a kind of band that characterizes the checkered ten to ten, making it easier to count the stitches at the moment of working the embroidery.

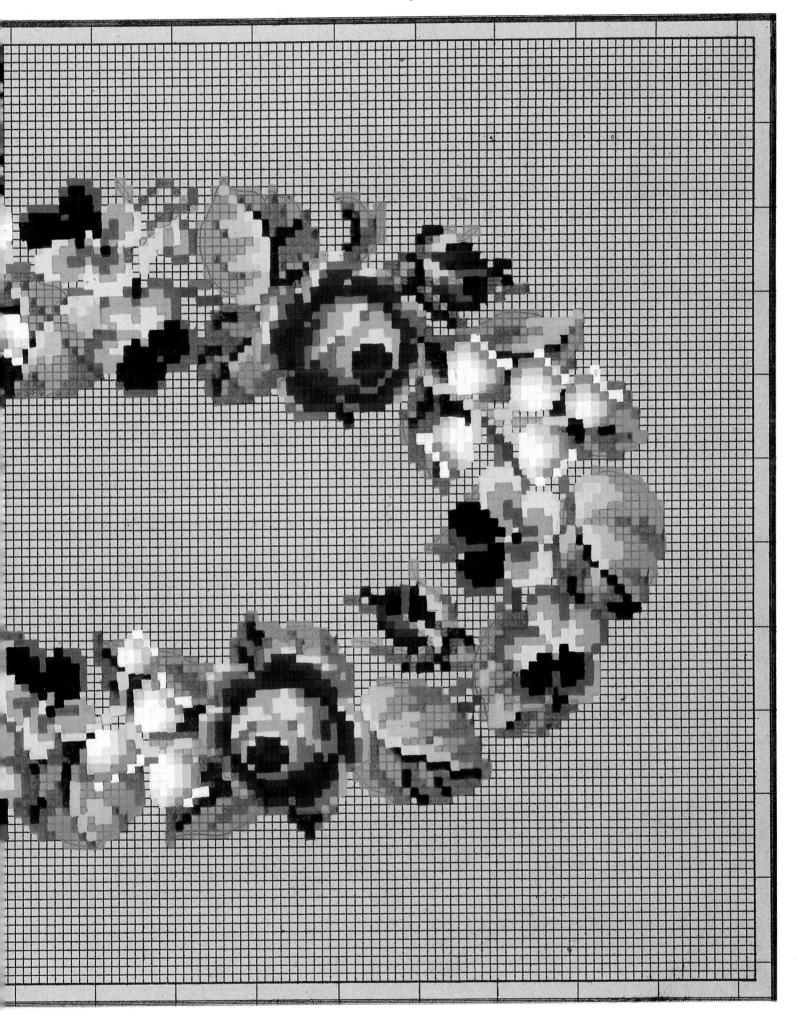

POPPY

Leaves

Cool Dark Green	●	501
Cool Green	◑	502
Cool Pale Green	○	504
Dark Green	◕	500
Green	⟍	3362
Pale Green	∟	3363
White Green	ǀ	3364

Flower

Red	⟍	304
Orange	×	349
Pink Salmon	∪	352
Pale Pink	.	754
Dark Violet	◣	550
Violet	ɯ	553
Pale Violet	s	554
Pale Lilac	□	211
Dark Sky-Blue	△	312
Black	■	310

This embroidery is shown on page 50.

WREATH

Leaves and branches			Flowers					
Black	●	310	Bordeaux	◣	902	Dark Fuchsia	△	915
Dark Moss Green	∩	935	Wine Red	B	498	Dark Pink	L	718
Moss Green	∀	520	Dark Red	‖	321	Pink	I	3608
Yellow Green	Q	731	Red	□	349	Light Pink	::	3609
Bronze Yellow	C	833	Vivid Pink	S	3705			
Dark Green Gray	0	502	Blue Violet	●	550			
Pale Green Gray	\	503	Deep Violet	◑	552			
Brown	✦	434	Violet	H	553	*The embroidery shown is*		
Dark Brown	⊙	801	Pale Violet	V	209	*part of the* sampler *illustrated*		
Orange	ε	738	White Violet	\	211	*on page 84*		
Yellow	.	725	Deep Fuchsia	■	814			

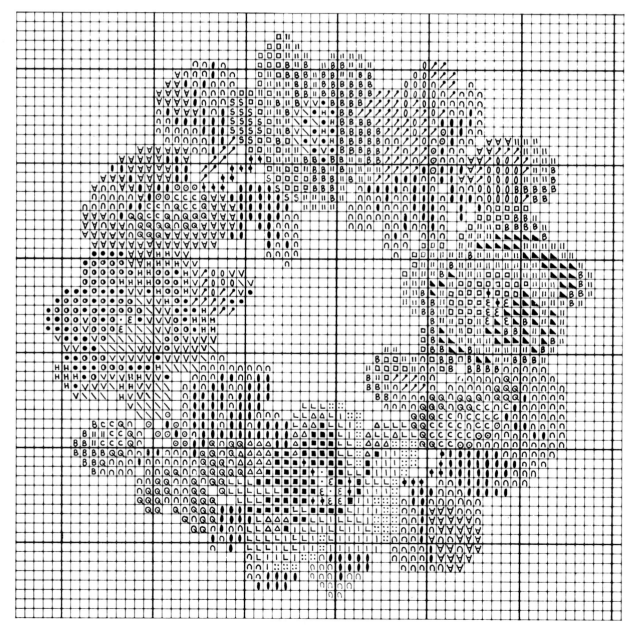

The garland is perhaps the most popular style of floral design in nineteenth-century embroidery: the types of flowers in the compositions vary, as does the combination of color and small touches, such as a ribbon or an inscription, but each of these garlands embodies the style and sensitivity of a century that loves to create within the harmonies of domestic life.

After publication of the first model for embroidery on
checkered paper in 1804, a wide diffusion of printed
sketches followed, collected in albums or published in
feminine magazines. With this development, a notable
homogeneity of production extends throughout all of
Europe which tends to end the differences found among
various countries as well as differences in the work done at
home for personal use and the work destined to be sold.

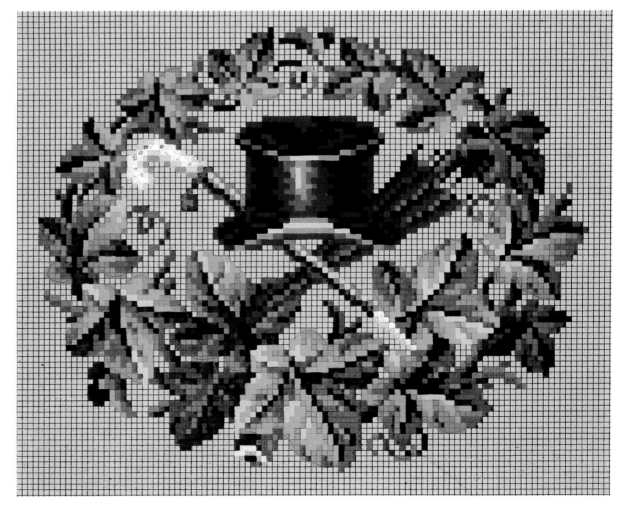

On these pages, three exceptional garlands contain
a bowler, a top hat with umbrella and baton and
the head of a horse. The first two were probably
designed for a specific use, perhaps to furnish a
men's hat shop.

Children and Animals

The Little Violin Player

«I won't invent a story, I wouldn't know how to invent anything as touching at that of a true story that I was told. It is about little Johnny, a marvelous, seven year old musician, that for three years had already become known throughout America. There was not a concert or performance where this child's picture wasn't shown.

Last month I also had a chance to see him for the first time; since then a day does not go by for me without seeing that sweet face and those big eyes, both smiling and melancholy at the same time...

Five years ago two small twins came to bring joy to my home. I would like to introduce them to you: as of now only a small number of friends know them; but because Charles has declared his intention to be a squire of the Circus one day, and Guy,

less ambitious, counts on becoming a
policeman, it is possible that people
will talk about them one day...
In the days of vacation (and
those days are frequent)
they are amused by various
things. They go to see
trained dogs, marionettes
and wonderful shows...The
other day, on Christmas eve,
didn't I find them crouched
in the kitchen with a big
pumpkin? Certainly they thought
that if they opened it, wheels would appear on either side, and that
the two kittens, intent on playing in the hallway with pieces of
onion, would immediately change into horses attaching themselves
to the carriage of Cinderella...

The last mime show performed this winter in the city of Boston was
particularly memorable for Charles and Guy... A bold prince went
in search of adventure in wonderland...

Then there was a fairy castle and then a cave of emeralds at the
bottom of a deep river; the scene changes were so rapid it was
astounding.

But it was young Johnny that was most interested in Charles and
Guy when he came to play the violin in front of the prince and his
fiancée...

His sweet face had that painful expression that is seen in all these
unhappy youngsters, not realizing that they are already old, seeming
to mix that in some strange way with their hair full of ringlets and
the rosy cheeks of a child from five to seven years old... ».

(The Aracne, February 1894)

RABBIT

Hedge
Black Green	❶	500
Dark Green	∪	501
Green	∟	502

Rabbit
Dark Green Gray	❟	3032
Pale Green Gray	V	613
Dark Beige	╲	437
Beige	○	738
Pale Beige	·	739
Brown	▲	433
Pink	◑	3608

The embroidery is a part of the sampler *illustrated on page 73.*

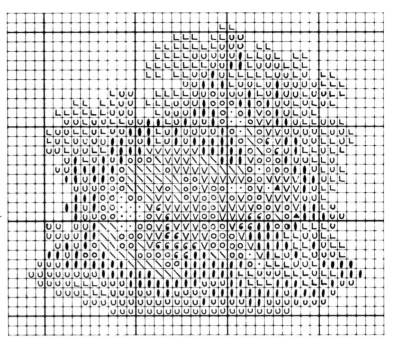

BRANCH WITH TWO BIRDS

Leaves			Bird on the right			Bird on the left		
Dark Moss Green	I	934	Dark Brown	❛	838	Dark Brown	❛	838
Cool Dark Green	U	501	Light Brown	❖	840	Light Brown	❖	840
Cool Pale Green	L	503	Dark Cord	╱	3012	Dark Hazelnut	╲	869
			Light Cord	❖	3013	Light Hazelnut	V	422
Fruits			Bordeaux	●	355	White Hazelnut	○	3047
Hazelnut	×	420	Hazelnut	×	420	Ecru		712
White Hazelnut	○	3047	Light Hazelnut	V	422			

The embroidery is a part of the sampler illustrated on page 73.

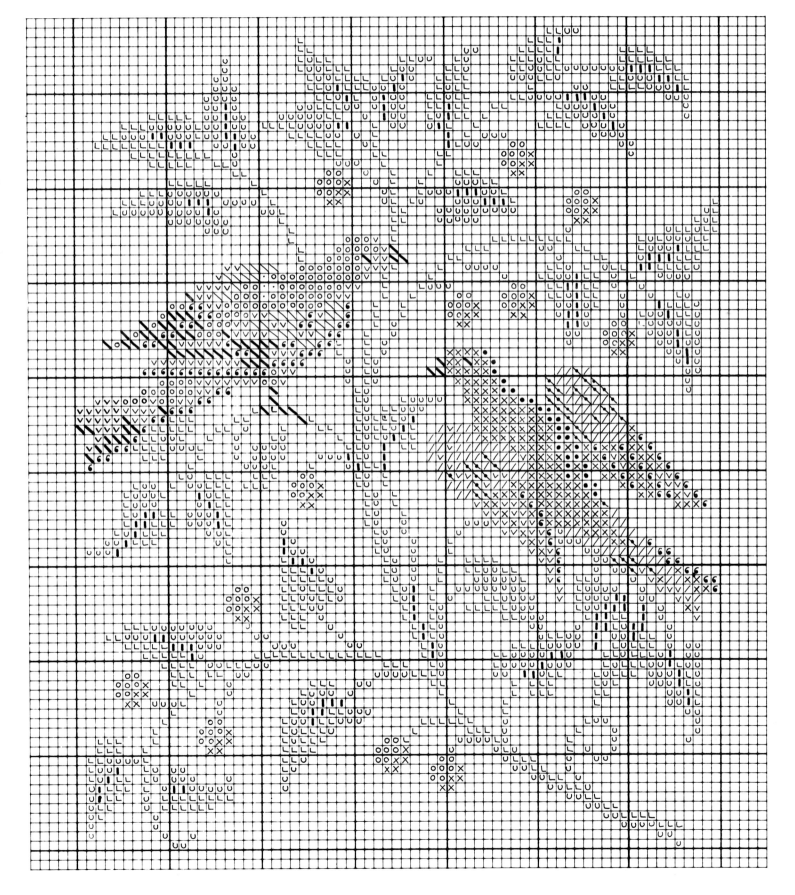

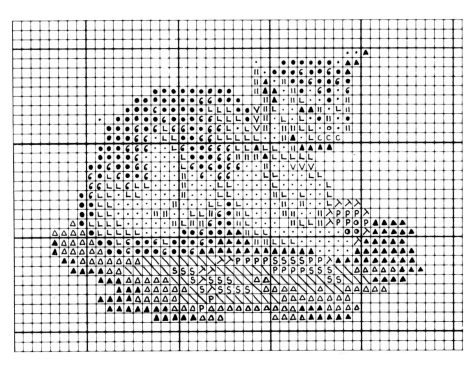

CAT

Kitten

Dark Gray	ʿ	645
Gray	‖	647
Light Gray	∟	3072
White	.	Neige
Chestnut Brown	▲	869
Dark Pink	C	3773
Pale Pink	○	3774
Blue	V	796

Small rug

Chestnut Brown	▲	869
Hazelnut	△	3045
Beige	S	3047
Ivory	⟍	746

Ball

Bordeaux	◑	3685
Vivid Pink	⟩	309
Pink	P	899

The embroidery is illustrated on page 91.

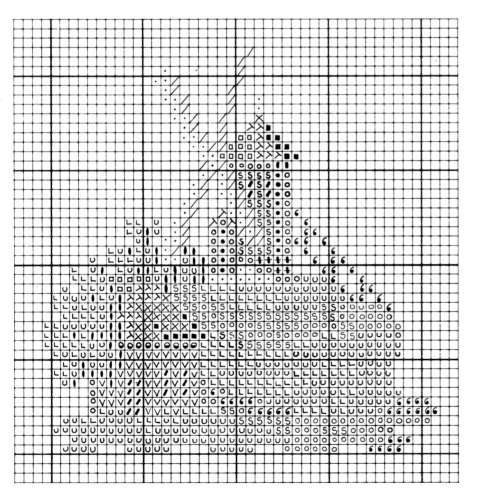

MILL

Dark Green	●	500
Green	∪	501
Pale Green	L	502
Dark Old Gold	ϭ	680
Old Gold	○	729
Light Old Gold	S	676
Very Light Old Gold	.	677
Gray Brown	/	372
Dark Gray	●	610
Gray Green	V	520
Dark Gray Green	◔	523
Yellow Orange	□	437
Light Brick Orange	⋋	435
Brick Orange	×	3045
Dark Brick Orange	■	370
Brown	⟋	3371
Light Brown	+	3781

The embroidery is a part of the sampler illustrated on page 73.

139

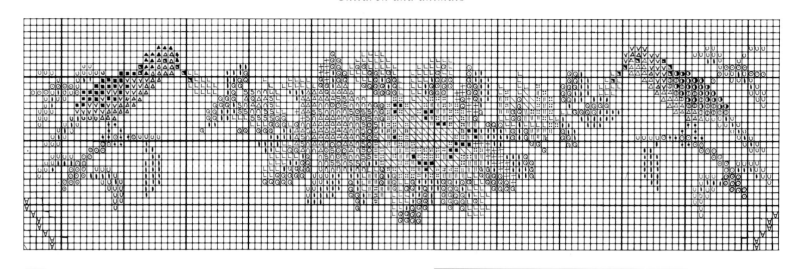

BIRDS WITH ROSE

Leaves and Branch

Black Green	I	500		
Dark Green	Q	319		
Pale Green	+	3347		
Light Brown	☉	433		

Bird on the left

Very Dark Coral Red	V	817
Magenta	■	815
Yellow	△	676
Black	◪	310

Flowers

Pale Yellow	H	677
Yellow	△	676
Dark Old Gold	S	680
Light Brown	☉	433
Magenta	■	815
Pink	::	335
Pale Pink	‖	3326
White Pink	\	818

Bird on the right

Light Blue	◑	824
Turquoise	Φ	806
Very Dark Coral Red	V	817
Yellow	△	676
Black	◪	310

The embroidery is on the flap of the purse illustrated page 66.

FOUNTAIN WITH BIRDS

Birds

White	•	Neige
Beige	○	822
Light Gray	◣	3023
Orange	₩	3776
Dark Blue	▼	939

Fountain

Dark Blue	▼	939
Dark Sky Blue	╱	311
Blue	Z	322
Light Baby Blue	╱	775

Earth

Brown	■	801
Chestnut Brown	▢	3781
Hazelnut	S	680
Dark Beige	L	676

Bushes

Black Green	●	934
Green	△	469
Light Green	U	581
Yellow Green	I	734

Rose

Dark Pink	◑	3778
Pink	×	945
Pale Pink	//	3770

Little Flowers

Dark Blue	╱	311
Blue	Z	322
Yellow	ɯ	725

The embroidery is part of the sampler illustrated on page 32.

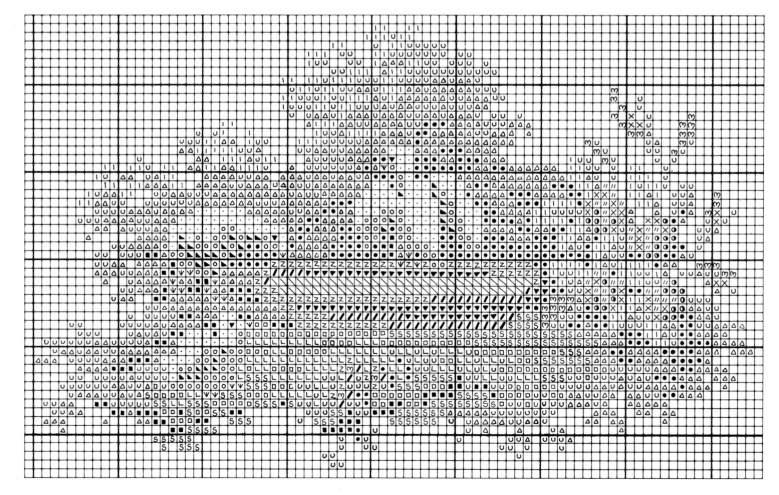

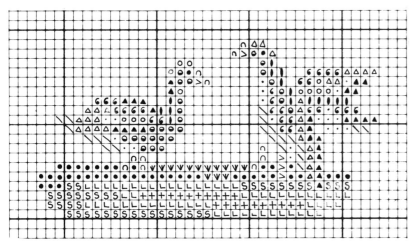

DUCKS

Duck			Earth		
Dark Green Gray	◗	500	Dark Brown	●	838
Green Gray	◖	501	Light Brown	Ⅴ	370
Dark Violet Gray	◗	3041	Gray	S	3051
Light Violet Gray	○	3042	Light Gray	L	3053
Dark Hazelnut	▲	869	Old Gold	+	677
Hazelnut	△	680			
Light Hazelnut	＼	422			
Ecru	·	3047			
Dark Yellow	>	729	*The embroidery is a part of the*
Light Yellow	∩	676	*sampler illustrated on page 73.*

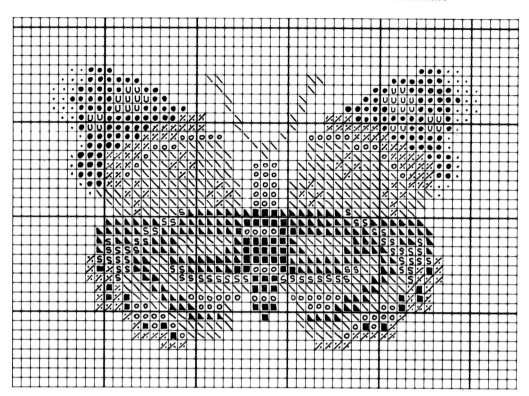

BUTTERFLY

Dark Brown	■	3371
Brown	●	801
Very Light Baby Blue	U	775
White Pink	.	754
Pink Salmon	⁊	3778
Yellow	\	676
Ecru	○	Ecrú
Blue	◣	824
Pale Delft	S	800

*The embroidery is a part of the
sampler illustrated on page 37.*

TWO BASKETS WITH A BIRD

Bows		
Red	✘	347
Dark Pink	╱	760

Stick		
Black Green	●	500
Green	U	3345

Bird		
Dark Yellow	○	726
Yellow	◿	3078
Light Yellow	\	746
Dark Gray	▼	318
Light Gray	ɯ	3072
Ivory	∧	712
Black	■	310

Basket		
Orange	▽	722
Yellow	L	725
Beige	✕	677

Leaves		
Green	U	3345
Dark Green	↖	890

Rose		
Red	✘	347
Pink	╱	760
Pale Pink	□	761
White Pink	.	819

Blue Flowers		
Blue	Z	3325
Orange	◑	352
Yellow	L	725

Orange Flowers		
Light Coral	◑	352
Peach Flesh	○	353
Black Green	↖	890

Violet Flowers		
Dark Violet	Ѵ	327
Light Violet	I	316

*The embroidery is a part
of the sampler illustrated
on page 48.*

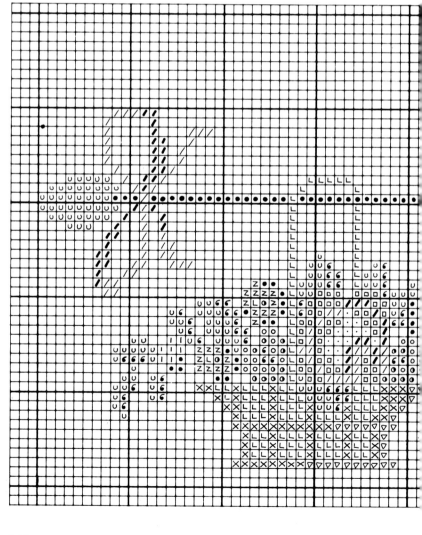

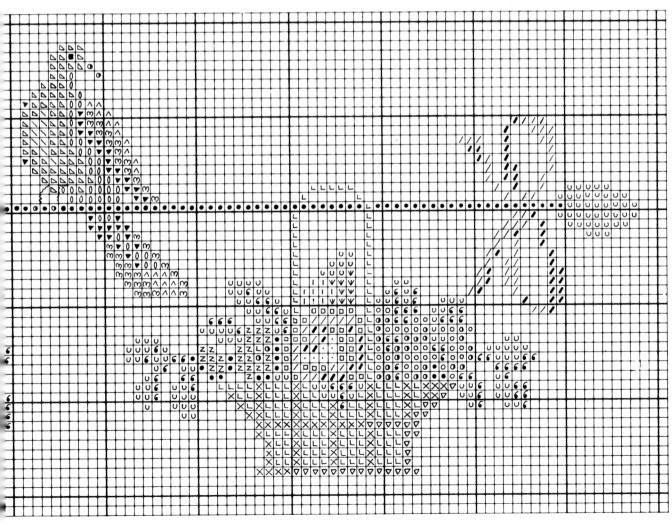

A very popular subject among the patterns of
embroidery were animals, often shown
together with children. Decidedly different is
the combination of animals inserted in the
geometric shapes among *the commedia
dell'arte* masks and costumed characters on the
next page.

The Hunt

The Seamstress

«Bent over her work from dawn till dusk
A young girl, pale and tired, remains.
At times the sun will kiss her golden mane
And yet at that kiss she doesn't smile
Nor hold her breath when the white moon
Appears through her closed chamber.
She descends from her small bed still tired
As soon as dawn begins to break.
Stitch by stitch she creates a fine
Embroidery that decorates rich fabrics and linen,
Wreathing feminine and soft
Monograms with faint flowers.
With each stitch an ardent desire
is stirred within her poor heart,
And on each stitch a thought crosses her mind
radiating of exceptional splendor.
Stitch by stitch her hands
Weave flowers while her mind wanders.

The young girl's vivid imagination
Weaves her sweet dream.
Embroidery and dreams bloom together,
But the roses of her face have faded.
A fog covering the sun can also cover all hope,
Like something glittering from faraway that might still occur.
Her hands are experienced in quilting
Brilliant linens, fabrics of silver and gold,
But her mind has become silent and drowsy
To joy and laughter from the heart.
And with the rising and setting of the sun, her needle
Shines in her slender, white hand.
Her embroidery is as a vague painting
Inspired by the gentle smile of spring.
But there is no sparkle in her eye: indifferent,
She studies her work and no longer admires the sky.
Stitch by stitch of life with her quivering heart
She wraps herself in a funeral veil».

Edvige Salvi *(The Aracne, February 1894)*

SQUIRREL

Meadow

Black Green	∪	501
Green	V	502

Squirrel

Dark Brown	'	433
Light Brown	L	434
White Brown 436	I	
Hazelnut	○	738
Beige	'	739
White	·	Neige
Black	●	310

The embroidery is a part of the sampler illustrated on page 73.

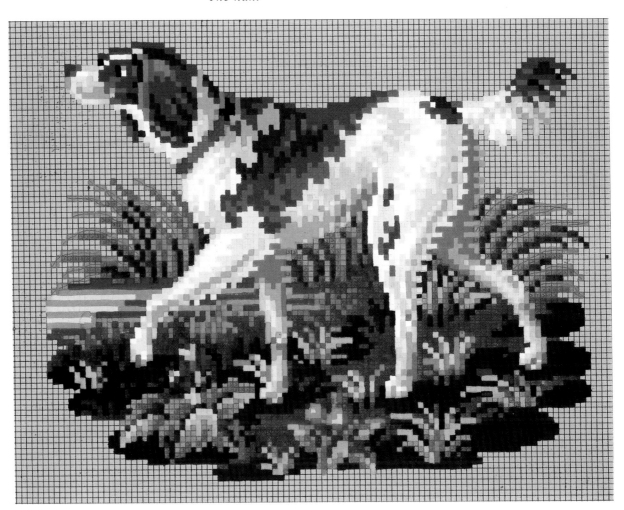

LANDSCAPE WITH COTTAGE

Trees and bush

Dark Green	●	935
Green	△	937
Dark Yellow Green	∪	732
Light Yellow Green	I	734
Dark Brown	■	3371
Brown	□	801

House and earth

Brick	◑	301
Dark Beige	∟	676
Beige	＼	3047
Dark Brown	■	3371
Chestnut Brown	×	839
Brown	□	801
Yellow	⋋	725

Lake

Very Light Sky Blue	·	3747
White Gray	V	3072

Boat

Brown	□	801
Brick	◑	301
Yellow	⋋	725
Blue	◤	322

The embroidery is part of the sampler illustrated on page 32.

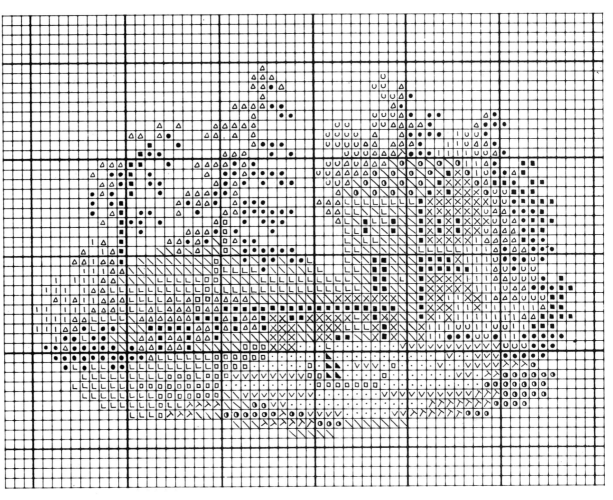

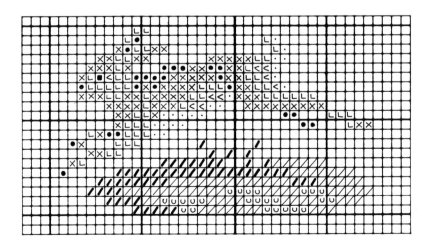

WILD HARE

Meadow

Dark Green	⁄	500
Pale Green	⁄	502
Beige	∪	422

Hare

Dark Brown	■	3371
Brown	●	898
Dark Hazelnut	L	3045
Light Hazelnut	×	3046
Light Yellow	·	3047
White	<	712

The embroidery is a part of the sampler illustrated on page 73.

HUNTING DOG

Dog			Earth		
Dark Brown	✎	838	Dark Green	●	890
Brown	＼	433	Green	∪	3345
Light Brown	×	434	Yellow Green	∟	581
Dark Cord	ᵚ	370	Dark Brown	✎	838
Light Cord	//	372	Brown	＼	433
Beige	.	644	Light Brown	I	869
Dark Gray	◣	413	Dark Khaki Green	I	3011
Dark Drab Brown	٠	611	Dark Hazelnut	Ѵ	680
White	□	Neige	Light Hazelnut	P	833

Collar

Red	◖	817	*The embroidery is*
Orange	⟩	3776	*illustrated on page 49.*

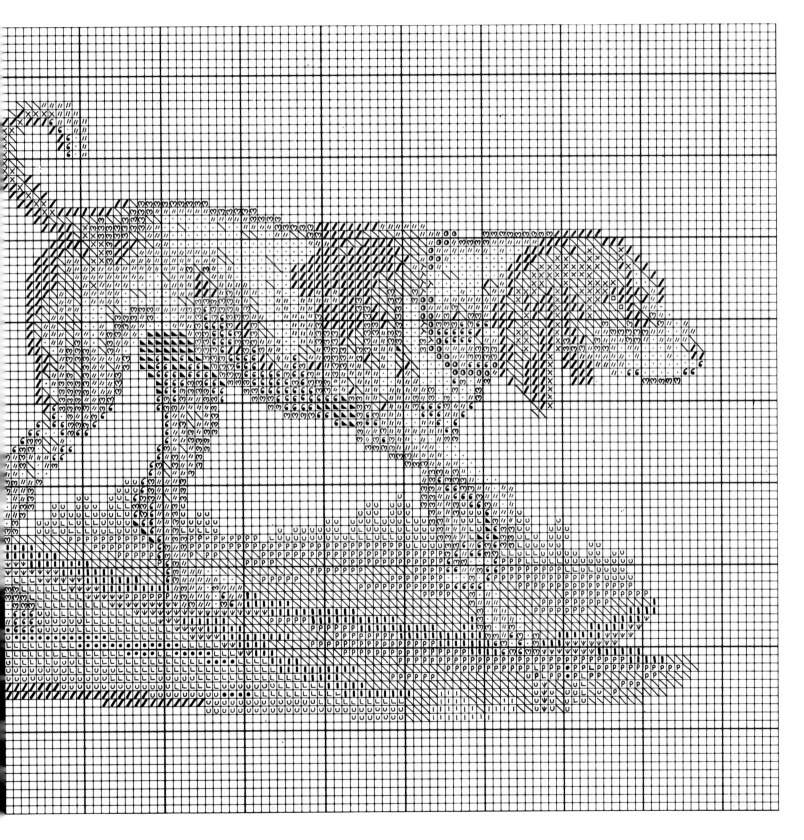

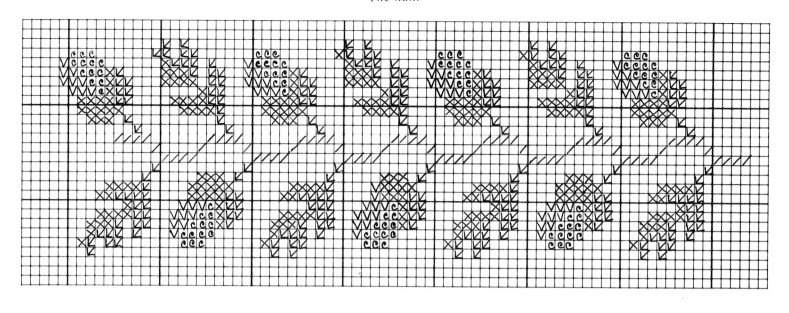

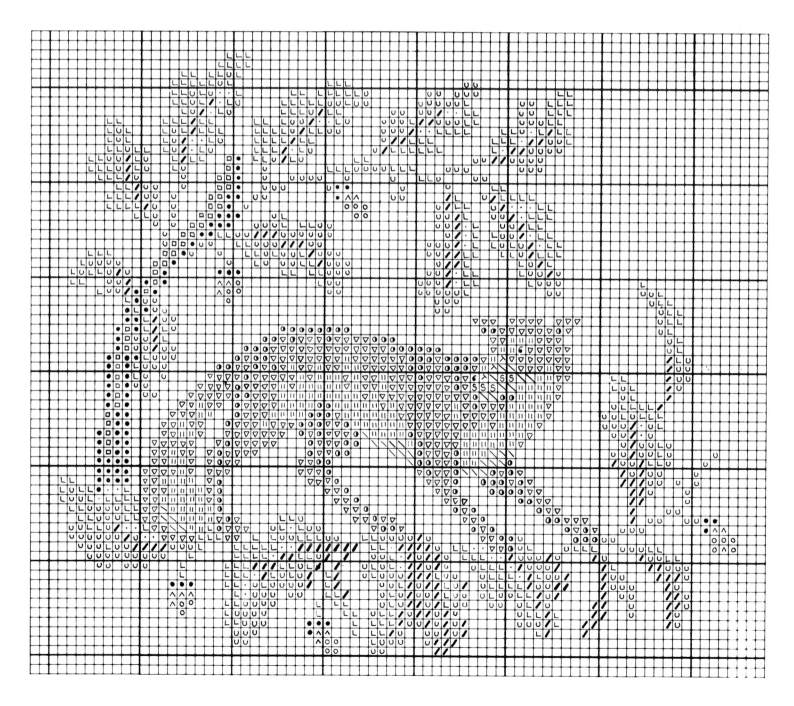

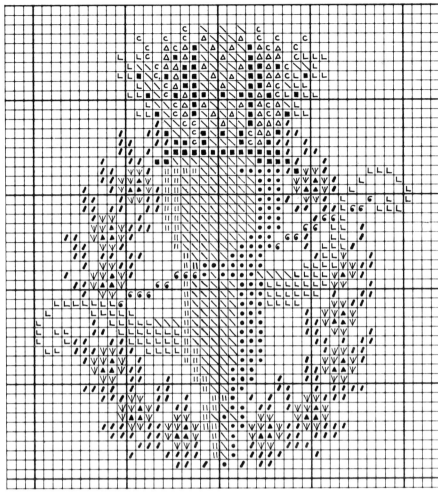

QUIVER

Leaves and flowers

Peacock Green	✕	501
Green Gray	ؙ	522
Pink	٧	945
Light Brown	▲	435

Quiver

Beige	△	739
Rosy Beige	＼	951
Chestnut Brown	●	3045
Brown	‖	422
Dark Brown	■	3371
Cool Hazelnut	∟	612
Light Hazelnut	C	420

The embroidery is a part of the sampler illustrated on page 73.

BRANCH WITH ROSE BUDS

Green	×	367
Dark Old Gold	↙	680
Brown	╱	434
Pale Pink	V	7.58
Rosy Beige	C	543

The embroidery is a part of the sampler illustrated on page 40.

FOX

Branches with acorns

Dark Green	I	500
Green	∪	502
Pale Green	∟	503
Light Yellow	.	3053
Yellow	∧	3046
Dark Brown	●	838
Light Brown	□	680
Chestnut Brown	○	420

Fox

Dark Ochre	◐	869
Ochre	▽	3045
Brick	‖	435
Ecru	＼	677
Black	ؙ	3371
White	⅄	712
Pink	S	754

The embroidery is a part of the sampler illustrated on page 73.

Borders

The little song of the needle

«I am a nimble needle, giving off sky-blue reflections, from the sharpest point, to the golden eye. I come and go, leaping, running on fabrics, on bright silks, on fluffy laces and on soft wools. With my bright and rapid quiver the mother of the family smiles, the young woman dreams and the old woman remembers or prays. Oh, pure blades of Toledo, oh, sparkling swords, I am, as you, made with the shiniest of steel; polished as you are, tempered as you are and leave a wound wherever I pass. But different from you - tools of death - I am a source of life. On velvets, brocades and flaxes whimsical flowers (missing only the perfume) bloom just for me. For me, the capes of monarchs, the sacred vestments of priests and the precious veils of maidens sparkle with gold and pearl. For me, everyone including the poor and the children, dress; they work and they gain.

I am poetry, comfort, gentleness and love.

I am the light-blue nimble needle, with the golden eye.

I am the needle that sews your white wedding dress, my young reader that sings my song».

Ida Baccini *(The Aracne, January 1893)*

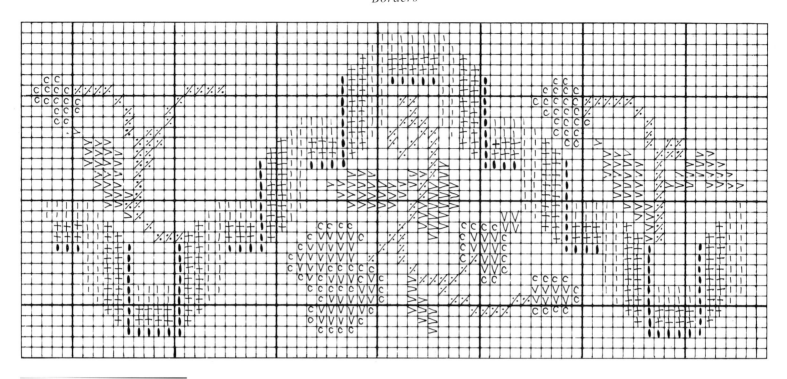

BLUE RIBBON

Blue	●	824
Sky Blue	+	800
Very Light Antique Blue	I	3753
Brass	⁄•	832
Pink	C	3779
Green Grass	>	3347
Dark Pink	V	758

The embroidery is a part of the sampler illustrated on page 20.

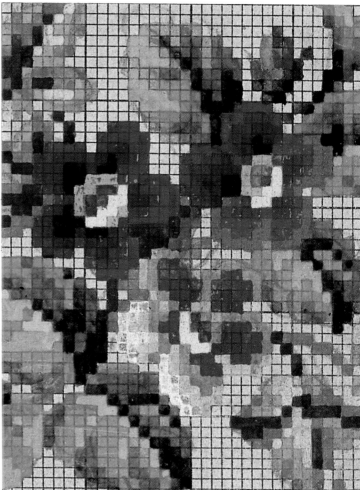

Above are two details of the border shown below. The enlargement allows for easier reading of the design and the organization of the colors in the individual squares. The more varied the range of hues and colors the more the embroidery seems real and soft.

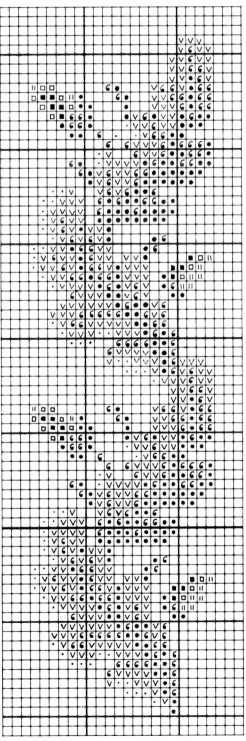

SMALL OAK BRANCH

Leaves

Dark Green	●	934
Green	ϟ	936
Pale Green	V	581
Pale Yellow Green	·	472

Acorns

Dark Coffee Brown	■	801
Light Brown	□	434
Beige	‖	738

The embroidery is a part of the sampler illustrated on page 72.

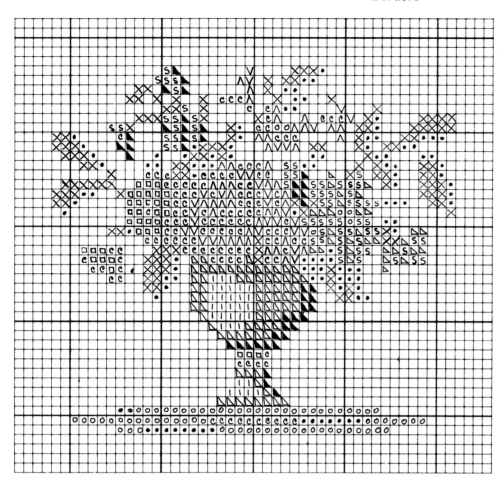

VASE OF FLOWERS

Dark Blue	◣	3750
Blue	◹	931
Light Blue	I	928
Light Yellow	◻	676
Rosy Beige	C	543
Old Gold	○	729
Dark Green	●	500
Green	×	367
Light Blue	S	775
Pale Pink	V	758
Pink	∧	948

*The embroidery is a part of the
sampler illustrated on page 40.*

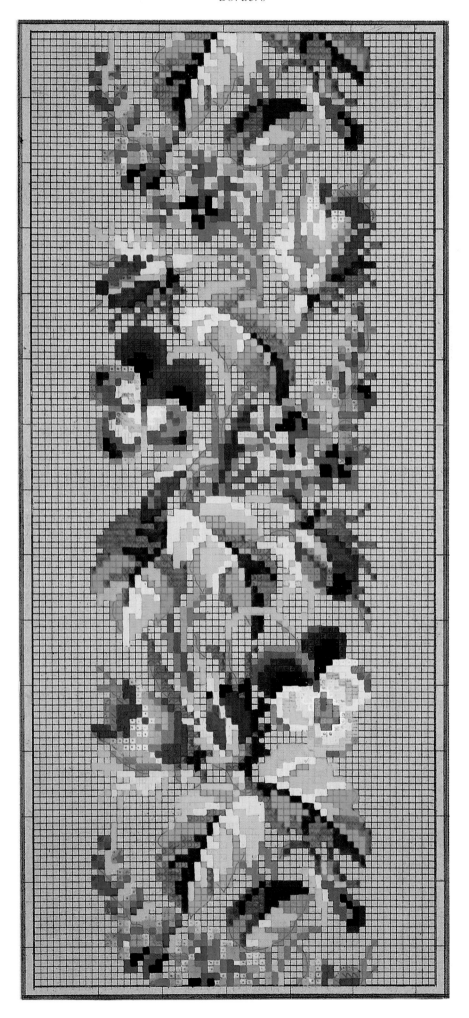

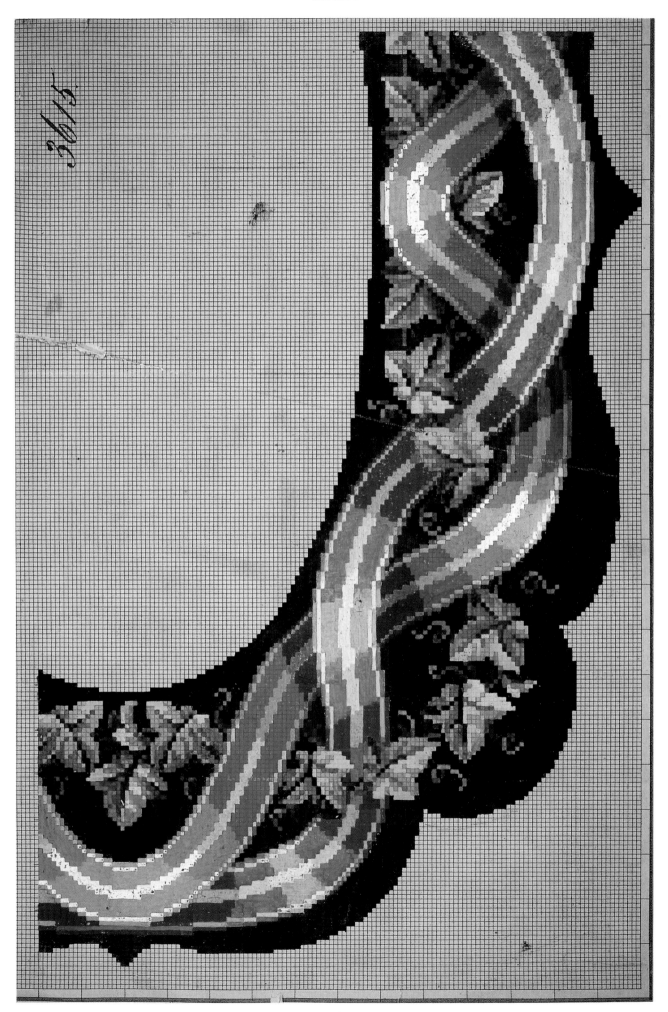

The borders conserved at the Kunstbibliothek of
Berlin are extremely varied in importance and size:
from the smallest, only a quarter inch high, to those of
eight to twelve inches, made for carpets, with
complex floral designs and braided ribbons.

Besides the albums of patterns that allow the adaptation of designs to different objects and fabrics, from 1851 there are also fabrics with the designs already printed, making it easier to embroider. But in general these kinds of patterns don't reach the type of quality of the embroideries that follow the paper sketch.

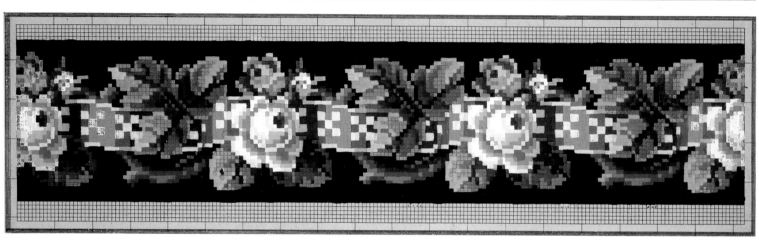

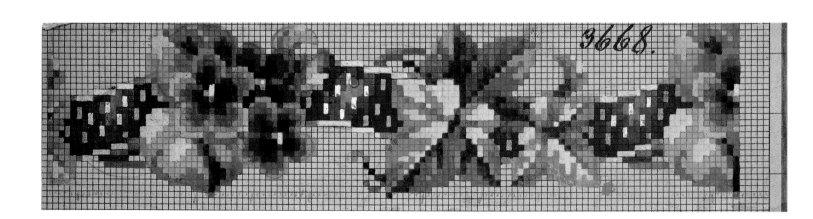

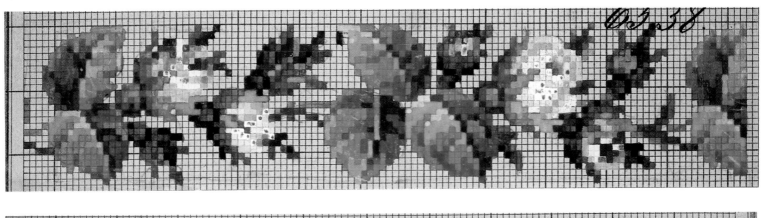

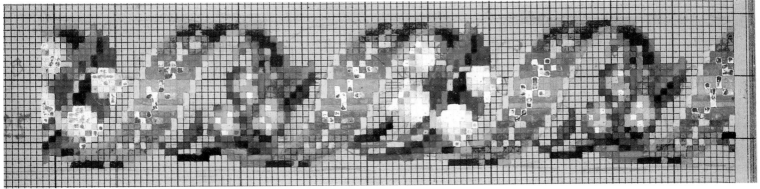

The embroidery done in *petit point* and cross stitch
in past centuries was generally worked on linen,
while in the nineteenth century it was also worked
on open weave hemp, cotton and on wide and
regular woven weft fabrics like the type of hemp
called "Penelope fabric".

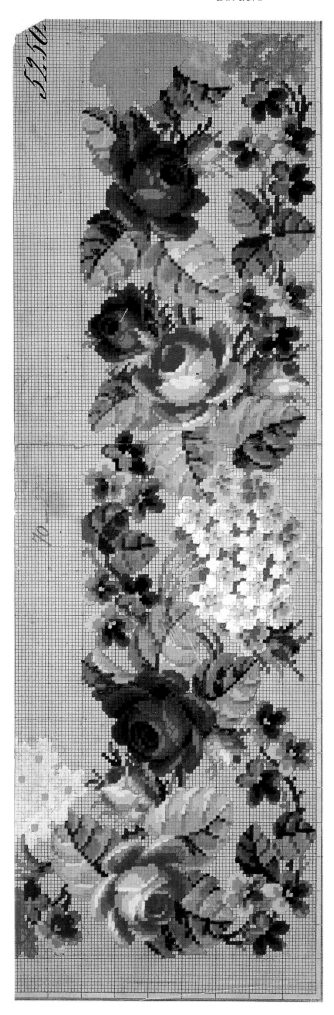

In the nineteenth century the most commonly used threads were of wool or silk (often woven together) and cotton. From 1856, after the discovery of aniline dyes, synthetic dyed threads appear, easily fading in the light, but allowing for an endless range of tones. With their introduction and diffusion throughout all of Europe, there are fewer differences in the choice of colors that previously characterized the production of the individual countries.

Pelmets

Useful Ideas

«How to copy sketches for embroidery onto fabric.
Working with white cotton (such as numbers, festoons, etc.) on a
plain weave cloth
*—To do a number of reproductions, it is better to copy the sketch
on transparent paper, to then glue it at the four corners over a
piece of thin, strong paper and then with a thin needle, following
the outline of the design, punch as many holes as possible into the
paper. The pin points will be visible, they can then be connected
with pencil, with rubberized blue ceruse or with a goose feather.
To remove the roughness that was left from the needle use a
smooth piece of pumice stone without corners, so that it doesn't
tear the sheet.*
Working with silk, satin, velvet and cloth fabrics.
*—The method is the same. Copy the sketch on transparent
paper, attach it in a way to a sheet of thin but strong white paper
so that it doesn't move. Then with a needle, punch holes to
follow the outline of the design. If the fabric is white, lightly dust it
with black powder, to simply trace the design. And if the fabric is
dark, dust it with sifted ash to trace the design. Mark the sketch
with a goose feather or a thin Martora brush dipped in rubberized
ceruse, or in rubberized blue ceruse, or with pencil if the satin is
light colored.*
Working with hemp cloth. *— If it is transparent put it over the
chosen sketch and then with a brush dipped in china or common
ink, copy the outline of the design. Be careful that the sketch and
the hemp cloth don't move and that they are both evenly placed. »*

E. Sandrone *(The Aracne, February 1893)*

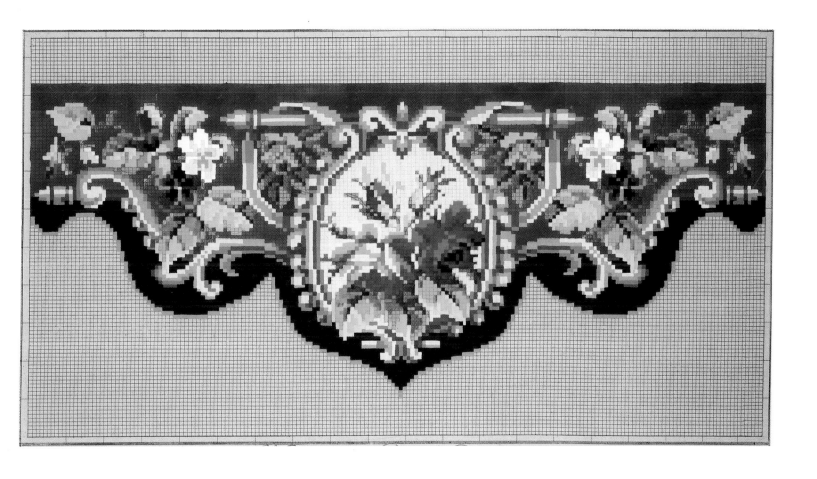

Extremely adaptable to various kinds of objects, the designs published in the albums offer the female imagination the possibility of embellishing their furnishings according to their own taste and style. In the nineteenth century (during the triumph of the bourgeoisie), the home becomes a mirror of the domestic life; a representation of everyday life.

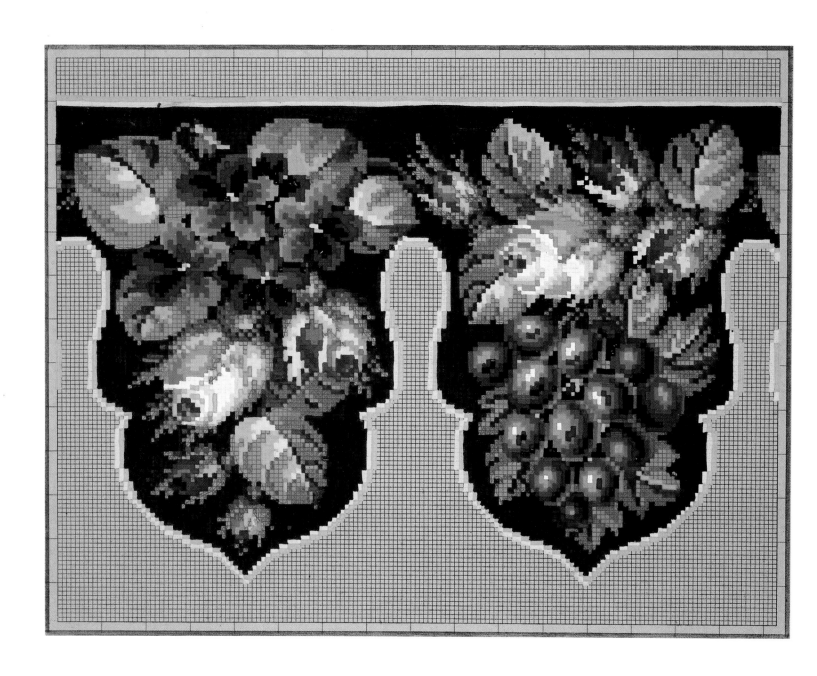

The pelmet is a very common element in the
furnishings of the bourgeois during the nineteenth
century, used to hide the mechanisms of the curtains
while offering at the same time, a decorative note.
They were draped and of rich fabrics, almost
always scalloped with elaborate outlines, in many
cases embroidered, most often with floral designs.

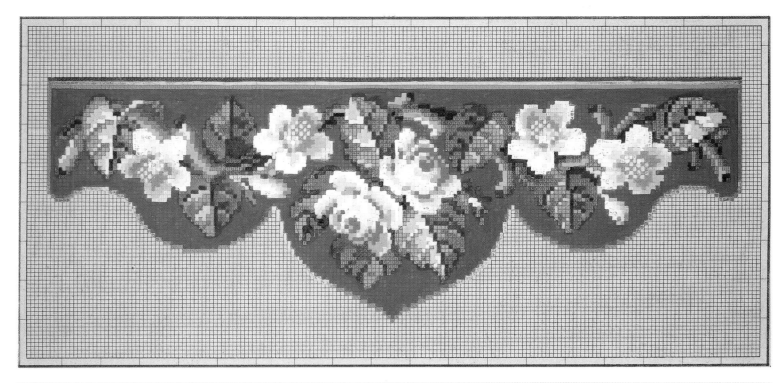

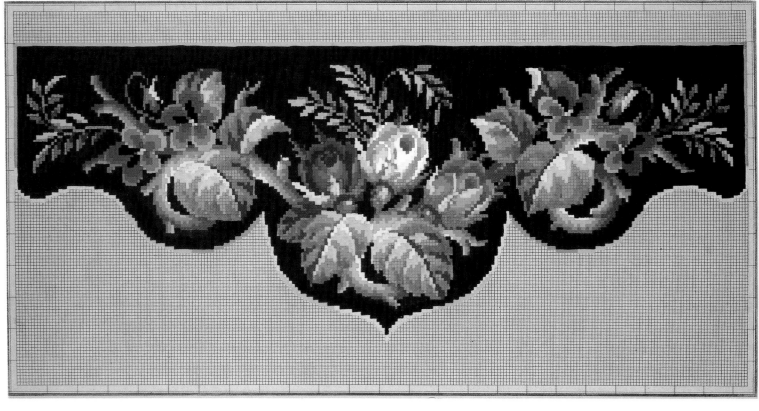

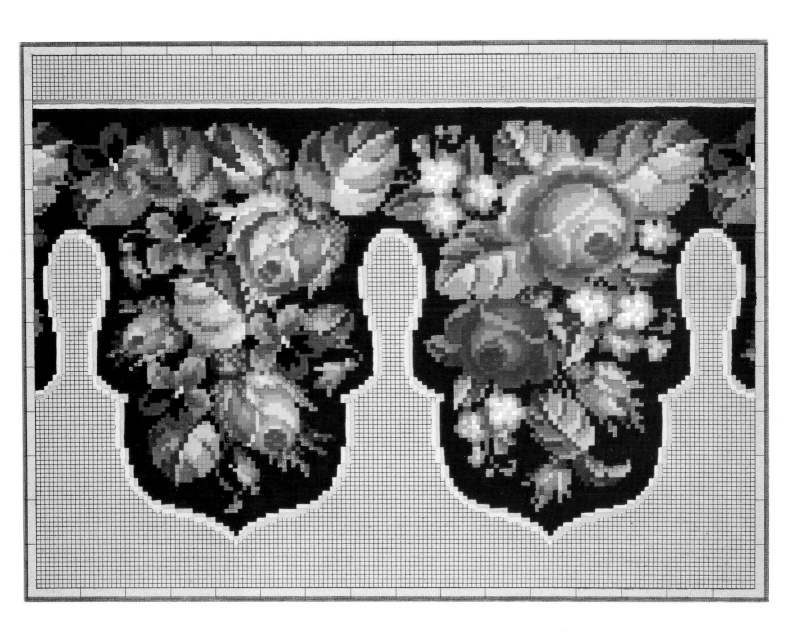

In the nineteenth century *Berlin wool work* had an
extraordinary success: embroidery becomes one
of the preferred pastimes of women in the new
bourgeois class who, freed from housework or the
necessity to work, had the time to devote to
reading, painting, music and to the pleasant and
patient activity of embroidery.

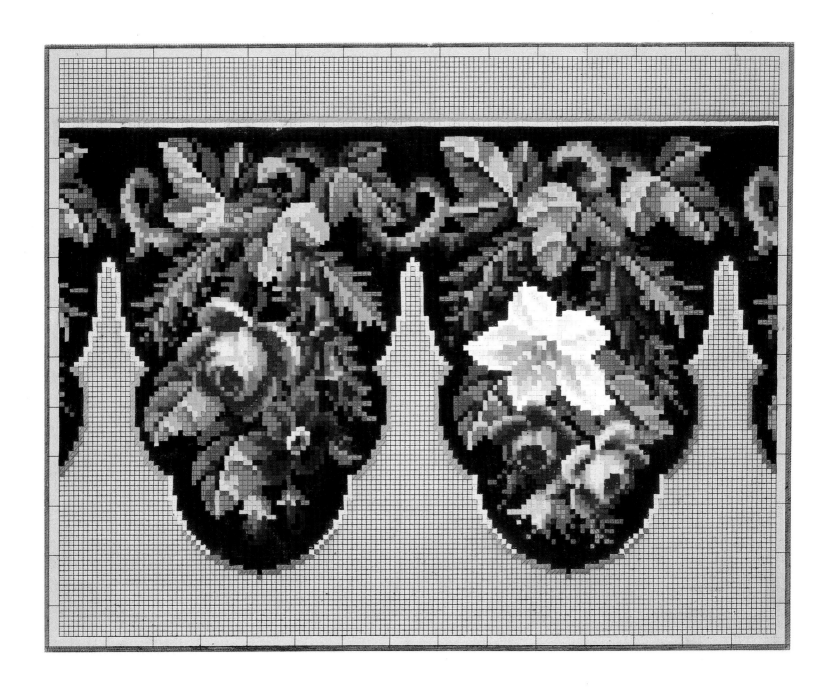

With the passing of the century *Berlin wool work* becomes more and
more successful; visible in the showing of female handiworks that spread
throughout all of Europe and America to eventually become actual
exhibits of domestic work. In the nineteenth century the rediscovery of
craftwork and of manual activity is brought to numerous professional
schools where not only is one technique taught, but where also a cultural
education is given, founding their style on the models of designers and
architects. In this same time period, generally connected to the schools,
the first museums dedicated to applied arts start to appear.

Rugs, cushions and tea cozies

Shades of Spring

«...The activity is a bit unclear, somewhat fading, slightly dried
from the cold winter and from the malificent seduction of the
funeral pall, reawakened and affirmed... It begins with the desire
to open the windows and to show those poor flowers to the sun
that the dust, smoke, lights and heaters have fatigued, as if in a
night-long vigil. The weak light begins to reveal the small
damages of the living room; crumpled cushions, old blankets,
dingy rugs, a stain in the carpet, a hole in the wallpaper to fix, a
smoke-stain in one cornet of the ceiling and the cracking of a
trinket that seemed intact.

Then the lady of the household becomes impatient and
somewhat fidgety, she thinks about changing this and redoing
that. Her knowing hands, wise and prepared, try to remedy
problems at first sight, investigate to discover others and then
realize that she no longer likes the position of the furniture. To the
women who want to do some renovation in their homes, I
recommend first that they visit their attic, basement or perhaps
even in an old barn nearby... maybe there they will find
something that sparks their interest.

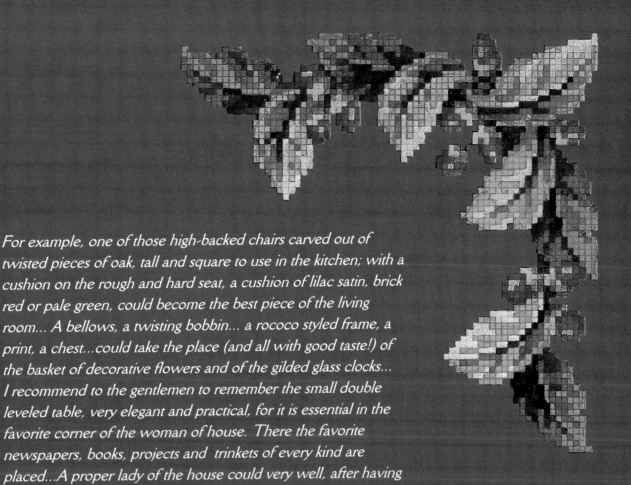

For example, one of those high-backed chairs carved out of twisted pieces of oak, tall and square to use in the kitchen; with a cushion on the rough and hard seat, a cushion of lilac satin, brick red or pale green, could become the best piece of the living room... A bellows, a twisting bobbin... a rococo styled frame, a print, a chest...could take the place (and all with good taste!) of the basket of decorative flowers and of the gilded glass clocks... I recommend to the gentlemen to remember the small double leveled table, very elegant and practical, for it is essential in the favorite corner of the woman of house. There the favorite newspapers, books, projects and trinkets of every kind are placed...A proper lady of the house could very well, after having found some pieces of unfinished wood, cover them herself, with felt or any simple type of cloth. They can also be quite attractive with the double levels covered with an embroidered design framed in dark velvet preferably, of which also the base would be covered. Some women hang a small purse on the side, impractical to use, but elegant and stylish to see».

Constellation *(The Aracne, March 1894)*

Two patterns for carpets with a rich center design framed by complex and elaborate borders are pictured on these pages. One of the reasons for the popularity of *petit point* is the similarity, in the final effect, between this type of embroidery and tapestries.

OAK BRANCH

Leaves			Acorns		
Black Green	●	835	Dark Brown	■	801
Dark Green	I	469	Dark Mustard	C	829
Green	∟	3347	Mustard	↘	831
Yellow Green	×	471	Moss Green	△	732
Yellow	V	472	Light Moss Green	∧	734
			Green Sage	//	3012
Branches			Light Yellow	·	3047
Dark Rust Brown	■	801			
Light Rust Brown	□	780	*The embroidery is shown on page 21.*		

In the designs for carpets and cushions the popular
theme was flowers, offered in countless variations that
have in common vivacity of colors and elegance of
composition. In the pattern on this page, the flowers
wrap in a S shape on a black background. This type of
background was rather common in *petit point* and
cross stitch in the middle of the nineteenth century,
showing off the embroidery well and in style with the
choice of furnishings from that time period.

An additional two floral patterns form very rich and
complex designs - in particular the pattern on the front
page distinguishes itself for its wide range of flowers
and colors and for the vividness of the composition.

One of the fundamental characteristics of nineteenth-century embroideries is the brilliance of the colors, evident in the designs for patterns. The bright coloring tends to emphasize the individual flowers rather than create the fine hues typical of the embroideries of the preceding century.

Among the countless objects that the nineteenth
century's fantasy knew how to transform with *petit
point* embroidery was the tea cozy; very common
in a century that emphasized the "tea ceremony"
in the course of a relationship. It was precisely
during the afternoon tea that women worked on
their embroidery.

On these pages two other typical half-circle
patterns for tea cozies are illustrated. It is interesting
to observe that noting the general naturalism of the
period, the design on the facing page is rather
stylized, including the shade of red on the large
leaves along the whole length of the ribbon. Also
the vivid blue in the background is quite unusual.

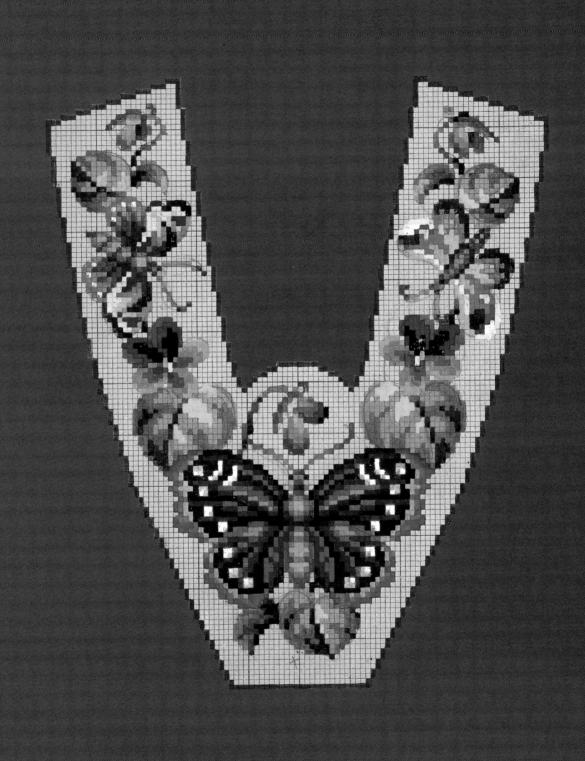

Purses, slippers, paniers

In the defense of embroidery

«...If embroidery is created with love and skill, it can become a substitute for art, almost as beautiful as art itself. It can sharpen the style, done by someone who cultivates it, with love of the knowledge of being able to do something beautiful, and satisfy their aesthetic tendencies.

Embroidery allows a woman, that has time but limited money, the luxury of being able to give something to her mother, sisters and friends, and in some occasions spare herself the mortification of being empty handed where it would be better to have something to give.

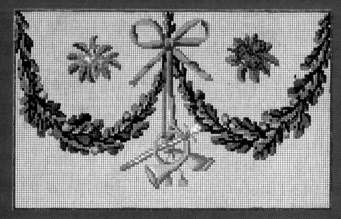

Knowing how to embroider well could be a good resource for a young teacher in a small town. But it is a different and special way that a fiancée embroiders the front of a shirt to give to her fiancé, a young mother embroiders any garment for her first child or that a loving mother creates some pieces for the hope chest of her only daughter... ».

Celestina Bertolini
(The Aracne, February 1893)

An irreplaceable and useful complement to a woman's outfit, purses are one of the more common accessories in the production of nineteenth-century embroidery, usually created with very fine thread and stitches and often embellished with gold threads or beads.

PURSE WITH FLOWERS AND BUTTERFLY

Border

Beige	•	677
Light Hazelnut	×	729

Butterfly

Light Hazelnut	×	729
Dark Hazelnut	◑	781
Topaz	ო	727
Very Light Mauve	＼	778
Very Light Baby Blue	I	3756
Dark Brown	●	3371

Scattered Flowers

Navy Blue	▼	312
Light Baby Blue	V	775
Pale Green	L	523
Light Yellow	ო	727
Red	،	347

Leaves

Dark Green	＼	500
Pale Green	L	523

First Flower on the Left

Light Hazelnut	U	758
Beige	P	951
Red	،	347

Second Flower (Bellflower)

Navy Blue	▼	312
Light Baby Blue	▽	3752
Very Light Baby Blue	I	3756
Light Yellow	ო	727
Light Hazelnut	×	729

Third Flower (Rose)

Red	،	347
Pink	╱	761
Light Pink	□	819

Fourth Flower (Carnation)

Light Hazelnut	×	729
Dark Hazelnut	◑	781

This embroidery is shown on page 46.

Characterized by the unmistakable V form of the upper, the designs for slippers are another recurrent theme in the albums of nineteenth-century patterns, at times also used to embroider children's booties.

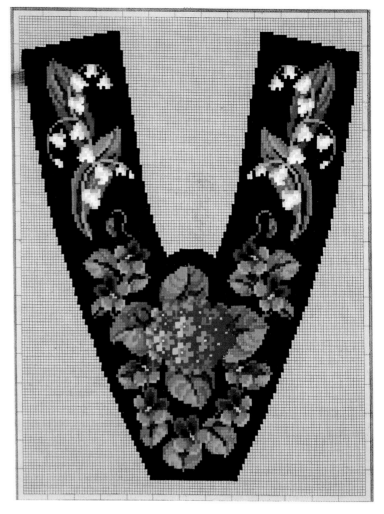

 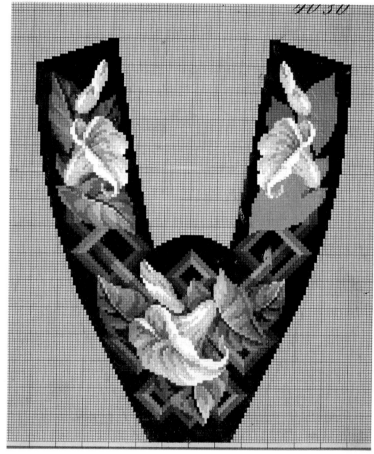

In this series of slipper patterns the floral design
is repeated, alone or with ribbons. Rather
unusual is the geometric background of the
design with callas on this page and the partial
pattern on the facing page with a branch of
coral on a Scottish plaid.

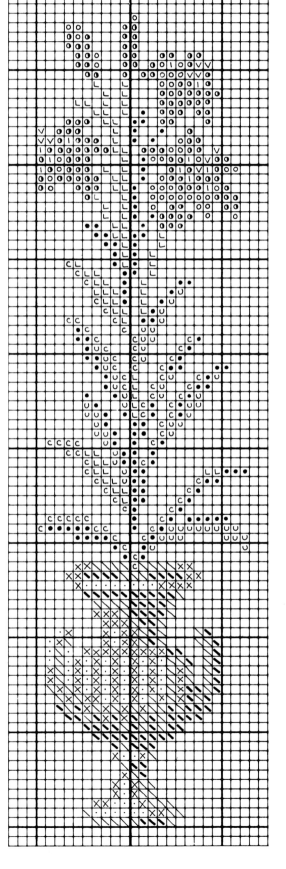

BRANCH OF LILIES

Vase

Brown Gray	❮	3787
Gray	＼	317
Very Light Antique Mauve	×	316
Lilac	.	3743

Leaves

Light Yellow Green	C	734
Dark Yellow Green	L	732
Pale Green	U	502
Dark Green	●	501

Flowers

White	○	Neige
Light Gray	◐	3072
Yellow	I	729
Very Light Baby Blue	V	927

This embroidery is shown on page 92.

FOX HEAD AMONG THE LEAVES

Ivy

Cool Black Green	I	500
Very Dark Jade	U	561
Jade	□	562
Light Jade	+	563
Warm Dark Green	●	895
Dark Forest Green	ɯ	987
Forest Green	Ѱ	989
Warm Pale Green	\	3348

Branches

Dark Brown	⁄	838
Light Brown	○	301

Fox

Dark Brown	⁄	838
Brown	▲	300
Light Brown	○	301
White Brown	II	976
Gray	◖	632
Light Gray	L	407
Rosy Gray	▽	543
White	.	Neige
Black	■	310

The pattern develops a detail of the side band of the design to the left.

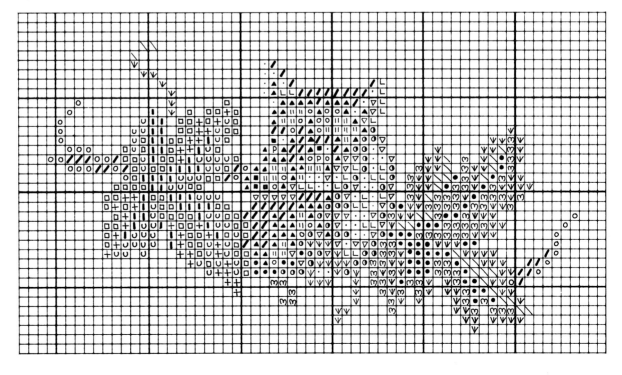

213

 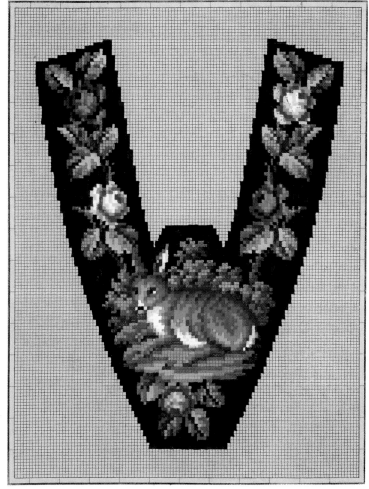

In these designs for embroidered slippers
animals are the main focus, the second most
popular subject after a floral designs. Rather
distinctive and certainly unusual is the design of
the dog holding in it's mouth a
slipper, shown on the facing page.

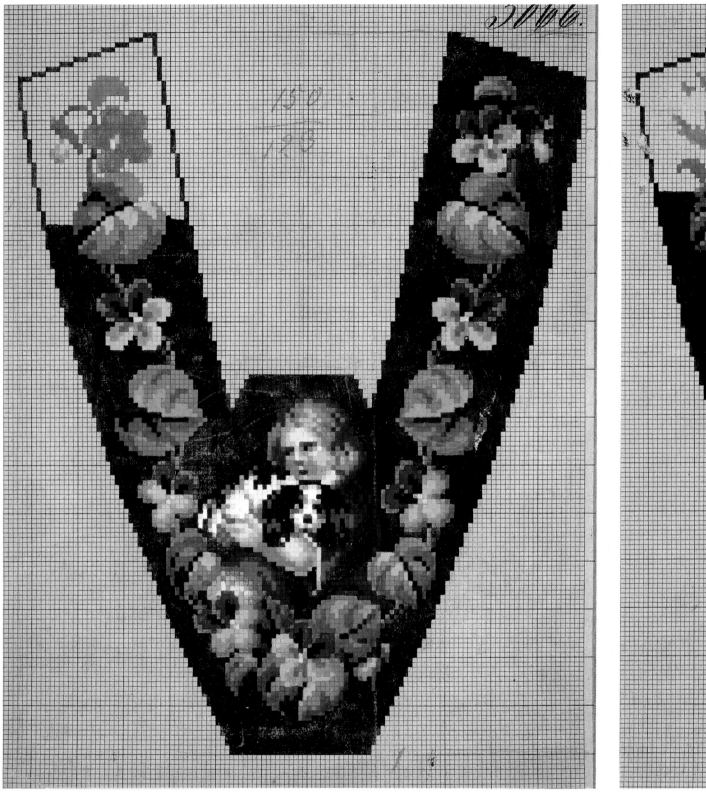

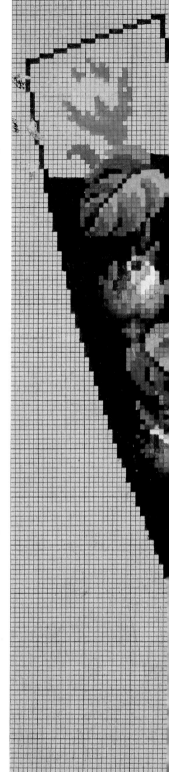

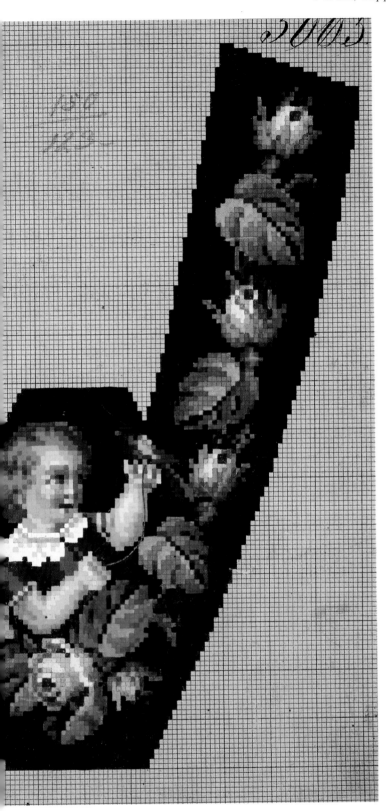

VASE WITH A SMALL ROSE BRANCH

Vase			Flowers		
Brown Gray	◣	3787	Dark Pink	■	3721
Gray	◥	317	Pink	∷	223
Very Light Antique Mauve	✕	316	Pale Pink	㎜	224
Lilac	.	3743	White Pink	▢	225

Leaves			
Light Yellow Green	C	734	
Dark Yellow Green	∟	732	
Pale Green	∪	502	*The embroidery is shown on page*
Dark Green	●	501	*92.*

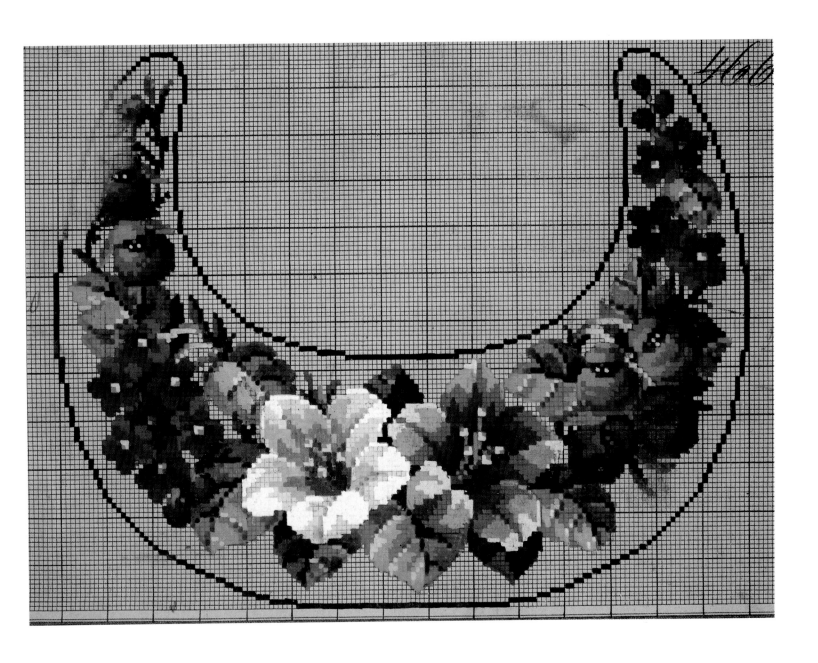

On the facing page is another design for a slipper,
most probably for a man, figured with the head of a
horse. Shown above is a pattern for a panier, a
female clothing accessory, consisting of a padded
crescent shape that was tied around the waist to
support the fullness of the skirts.

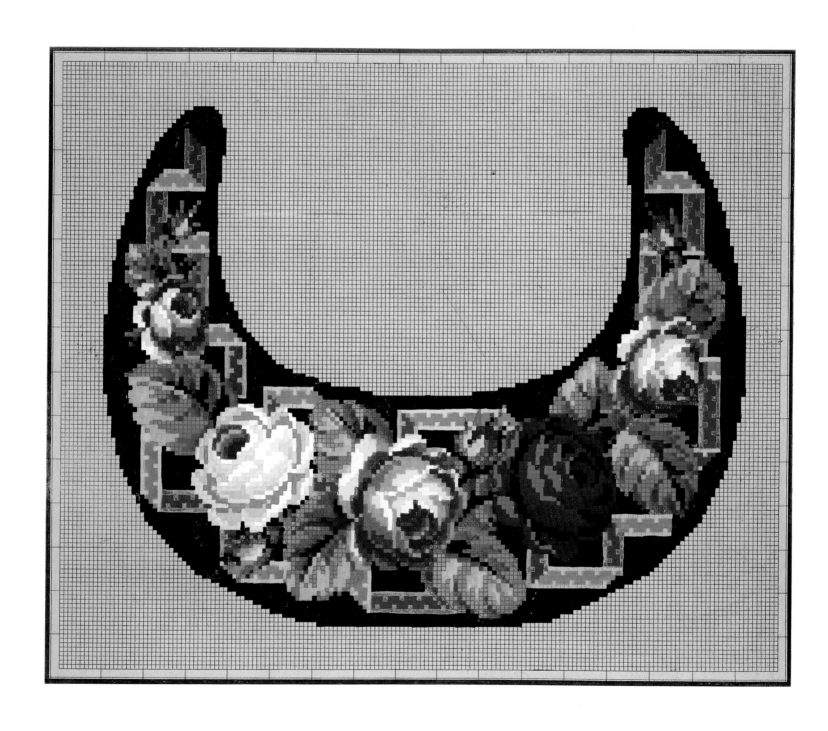

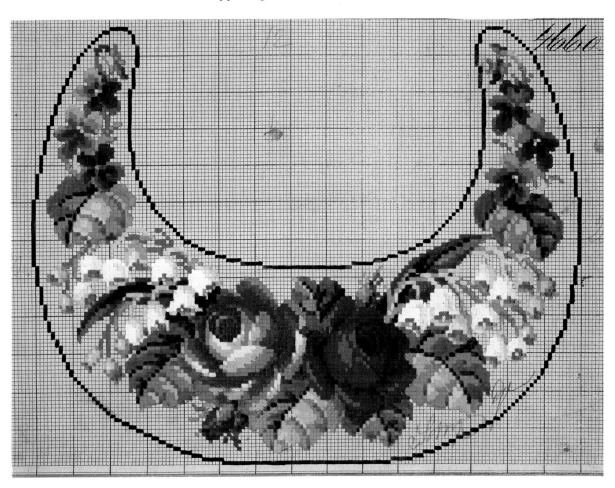

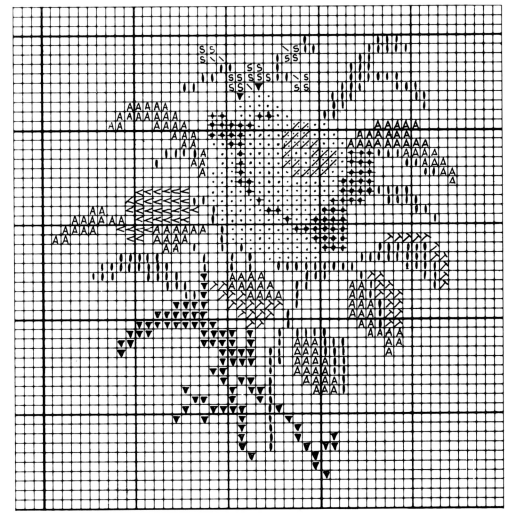

ROSE

Light Baby Blue	S	800
Yellow	＼	676
Green	●	991
Dark Green	▼	500
White Pink	.	754
Pale Pink	✦	758
Pink Salmon	⁄.	3778
Mustard	A	832
Brass	＞	680
Dark Topaz	<	782

This embroidery is a part of the sampler illustrated on page 37.

221

Bibliography

M. Abegg, A propos Patterns for Embrodery, Lace and Woven Textiles, Berna, 1978.

L. Ashton, *Samplers Selected and Described*, London-Boston, 1926.

J. Berman, C. Lazarus, *The Glorafilia Needlepoint Collection*, s.d.

E. Bradley, *Decorative Victorian Needlework*, London, 1990.

M. Carmignani, *Merletti a Palazzo Davanzati. Manifatture europee dal XVI al XIX secolo*, catalogo della mostra, Firenze, 1981.
[*Lace at Palazzo Davanzati. European Handiwork from the XVIth to XIXth century*, catalogue from the exhibit, Florence, 1981]

M. Carmignani, *Imparaticci = Samplers. Esercizi di ricamo delle bambine europee ed americane dal Seicento all'Ottocento*, catalogo della mostra, Firenze, 1986.
[*Samplers. Embroidery exercises from European and American children from the Seventeenth to the Nineteenth Century*, catalogue from the exhibit, Florence, 1986]

E. Celesia, *Scuole Professionali Femminili*, Genova, 1871.
[*Professional Girl's Schools*, Genova, 1871]

P. Clabburn, *Masterpieces of Embroidery*, Oxford, 1981.

R. Deforges, G. Dormann, *Il libro del punto croce*, Milano, 1988.
[*The Book of Cross-Stitch*, Milan, 1988]

R. Deforges, G. Dormann, *Punto croce creativo*, Milano, 1989.
[*Creative Cross-Stitch*, Milan, 1989]

Th. de Dillmont, *Enciclopedia dei lavori femminili*, Milano, 1989.
[*Encyclopedia of Women's Work*, Milan, 1989]

M. Dobry, *Tappichstickerei - Vorlagen, Material, Arbeisanleitung*, Zurigo, 1979.

J. Edwards, *Crewel Embroidery in England*, New York, 1975.

M. Eirwen Jones, *English Crewel Designs*, London, 1974.

M. Fawdry, D. Brown, *The book of Samplers*, Guilford-London, 1980.

N. von Gockerell, *Stickmustertücher. Kataloge des Bayerischen Nationalmuseum*, Monaco, 1980.

E. H. Gombrich, Il senso dell'ordine. Studio sulla psicologia dell'arte decorativa, Torino, 1984.
[The Sense of Order. Study of the Psychology of Decorative Arts, Turin, 1984]

M. Huish, *Samplers & Tapestry Embroideries*, New York, 1970 (1st ed. 1900).

C. Humphrey, *English Samplers at the Fitzwilliam*, Cambridge, 1984.

P. Johnstone, *Turkish Embroidery*, London, 1985.

P. Johnstone, *Three Hundred Years of Embroidery 1600-1900*, Richmond, 1987.

A. Kendrick, *English needlework*, London, 1933.

D. King, *Samplers*, catalogo della mostra, London, 1960.
[*Samplers*, catalogue from the exhibit, London, 1960]

S. M. Levey, *Discovering Embroidery of the 19th century*, Aylesbury, 1971.

M. Merrit Horne, *The Story of Samplers*, Filadelfia, 1963.

Mostra del Tessile Nazionale, Scuole Professionali tessili, catalogo della mostra, Roma, 1933.
[*Exhibit of National Textiles, Professional Textile Schools*, catalogue from the exhibit, Rome, 1933

T. Naomi, *Samplers in the Royal Scottish Museum*, Edinburgh, 1978.

J. L. Nevinson, *Catalogue of English Domestic Embroidery of the Sixteenth and Seventeenth centuries*, London, 1950.

G. Ostaus, *La vera perfezione del disegno per punti e ricami*, Bergamo, 1901 (1st ed. 1561).
[*The True Perfection of Designs for Stitches and Embroidery*, Bergamo, 1901 (First edition 1561)]

P. A. Paganino, *Il Burato - Libro dei ricami*, Venezia, 1530.
[*Il Burato - The Book of Embroidery*, Venice, 1530]

F. Pieroni Bortolotti, *Alle origini del movimento femminile*, Torino, 1975.
[*The Origins of the Feminist Movement*, Turin, 1975]

M. G. Proctor, *Victorian Canvas Work, Berlin Wool Work*, London, 1972.

J. L. Santoro, *Paesaggio e natura morta nell'arte tessile tra Sei e Settecento*, Firenze, s.d.
[*Landscape and Still Life in Textile Arts between the Seventeenth and Eighteenth Century*, Florence, s.d.]

A. Sebba, *Samplers. Five centuries of a gentle craft*, New York, 1979.

L. Synge, *Antique Needlework*, Dorset, 1982.

L. Tillet, *American Needlework 1776-1976. Needlepoint and Crewel Patterns Adapted from Historic American Images* (premessa di Rose Kennedy), Boston, 1987.

F. Vinciolo, *Les singuliers et nouveaux pourtraicts*
du signeur Federic de Vinciolo Venitien,
pour toutes sortes d'ouvrages de Lingerie.
Dedié à la royne douairière de France de rechef
et pour la troisième fois augmentez, outre le réseau premier
et le point couppéet lacis, de plusieurs beaux
et differents portass de réseau de pointconté, avec le nombre
des mailles, chose non encore venëny inventée.
A Paris pour Jean le Clerc, Bergamo, 1909 (1st ed. Parigi, 1587).

The photographs in this volume were given by the quoted Museums and from: A. Dagli Orti: 6, 50, 51, 52a-b, 53, 54, 55, 56a-b, 57, 58, 58, 60, 61a-b, 62, 63, 64, 65, 66a-b, 67, 68; G. Dagli Orti: 2; Kiemer: 26; M. Quattrone: 0, 21, 35, 37, 40, 45, 46, 47, 48, 49, 69, 70, 71; L. Sully Jaulmes: 43.